THE PARTHIAN STATIONS
OF ISIDORE OF CHARAX

Wipf and Stock Publishers
199 W 8th Ave, Suite 3
Eugene, OR 97401

Parthian Stations by Isidore of Charax
An Account of the Overland Trade Route Between the Levant and India
in the First Century B. C.
By Schoff, Wilfred H.
Softcover ISBN-13: 978-1-6667-7314-9
Hardcover ISBN-13: 978-1-6667-7315-6
eBook ISBN-13: 978-1-6667-7316-3
Publication date 3/7/2023
Previously published by Commercial Museum, 1914

This edition is a scanned facsimile of the original edition published in 1914.

The illustration on the title page is of a tetradrachm of Tiridates II in the Parthian Collection of the British Museum.

PARTHIAN STATIONS
BY
ISIDORE OF CHARAX

AN ACCOUNT OF THE OVERLAND
TRADE ROUTE BETWEEN THE
LEVANT AND INDIA IN THE
FIRST CENTURY B. C.

THE GREEK TEXT, WITH A TRANSLATION
AND COMMENTARY
BY
WILFRED H. SCHOFF, A. M.
Secretary of the Commercial Museum, Philadelphia

WIPF & STOCK · Eugene, Oregon

ΙΣΙΔΩΡΟΥ ΧΑΡΑΚΗΝΟΥ ΣΤΑΘΜΟΙ ΠΑΡΘΙΚΟΙ

Μεσοποταμίας καὶ Βαβυλωνίας σχοῖνοι ροα'.
Ἀπολλωνιάτιδος σχοῖνοι λγ'.
Χαλωνίτιδος σχοῖνοι κα'.
Μηδίας σχοῖνοι κβ'.
Καμβαδηνῆς σχοῖνοι λα'.
Μηδίας τῆς ἄνω σχοῖνοι λη'.
Ῥαγιανῆς Μηδίας σχοῖνοι νη'.
Χοαρηνῆς σχοῖνοι ιθ'.
Κομισηνῆς σχοῖνοι νη'.
Ὑρκανίας σχοῖνοι ξ'.
Ἀσταυηνῆς σχοῖνοι ξ'.
Παρθυηνῆς σχοῖνοι κε'.
Ἀπαυαρκτικηνῆς σχοῖνοι κζ'.
Μαργιανῆς σχοῖνοι λ'.
Ἀρείας σχοῖνοι λ'.
Ἀναυῆς σχοῖνοι νε'.
Ζαραγγιανῆς σχοῖνοι κα'.
Σακαστανῆς σχοῖνοι ξγ'.
Ἀραχωσίας σχοῖνοι λς'.
Ὁμοῦ σχοῖνοι ωνη'.

Μεσοποταμίας καὶ Βαβυλῶνος σχοῖνοι ροα'.

1. Διαβάντων τὸν Εὐφράτην κατὰ τὸ Ζεῦγμα, πόλις ἐστὶν Ἀπάμεια, εἶτα Δαίαρπ κώμη. Ἀπέχει δὲ Ἀπαμείας καὶ τοῦ Εὐφράτου ποταμοῦ σχοίνους γ'. Εἶτα Χάραξ Σίδου, ὑπὸ δὲ Ἑλλήνων Ἀνθεμουσιὰς πόλις, σχοῖνοι ε'· μεθ' ἣν Κοραία ἡ ἐν Βατάνῃ, ὀχύρωμα, σχοῖνοι γ'.

PARTHIAN STATIONS

By Isidore of Charax

Through Mesopotamia and Babylonia	171	Schoeni
" Apolloniatis	33	"
" Chalonitis	21	"
" Media	22	"
" Cambadena	31	"
" Upper Media	38	"
" Media Rhagiana	58	"
" Choarena	19	"
" Comisena	58	"
" Hyrcania	60	"
" Astauena	60	"
" Parthyena	25	"
" Apauarticena	27	"
" Margiana	30	"
" Aria	30	"
" Anaua	55	"
" Zarangiana	21	"
" Sacastana	63	"
" Arachosia	36	"
Total	858	Schoeni
Mesopotamia and Babylonia	171	Schoeni

1. For those who cross the Euphrates, next to Zeugma is the city of Apamia, and then the village of Daeara. It is 3 schoeni distant from Apamia and the river Euphrates. Then Charax Sidae, called by the Greeks the city of Anthemusias, 5 schoeni: beyond which is Coraea, in Batana, a fortified place: 3 schoeni. To the right of this place is Mannuorrha Auyreth, a fortified place, and a well, from which the inhabitants get drinking water, 5 schoeni. Then Commisimbela, a fortified place: by which flows the river Bilecha, 4 schoeni. Then

Ἐν δεξιοῖς ταύτης Μαννούορρα Αὐυρὴθ, ὀχύρωμα καὶ κρήνη, ἐξ ἧς ἄρδουσιν οἱ ἐγχώριοι, σχοῖνοι ε΄. Εἶτα Κομμισίμβηλα ὀχύρωμα· παραρρεῖ δὲ ποταμὸς Βίληχα, σχοῖνοι δ΄. Εἶτα Ἄλαγμα ὀχύρωμα, σταθμὸς βασιλικός, σχοῖνοι γ΄· μεθ' ὃν Ἴχναι πόλις Ἑλληνὶς, Μακεδόνων κτίσμα· κεῖται δ' ἐπὶ Βάλιχα ποταμοῦ, σχοῖνοι γ΄. Εἶτα Νικηφόριον παρ' Εὐφράτην πόλις Ἑλληνὶς, κτίσμα Ἀλεξάνδρου βασιλέως, σχοῖνοι ε΄. Ἔνθεν παραποταμία Γαλάβαθα, κώμη ἔρημος, σχοῖνοι δ΄. Εἶτα Χουμβανὴ κώμη, σχοῖνος α΄· ἔνθεν Θιλλάδα Μιρράδα, σταθμὸς βασιλικός, σχοῖνοι δ΄. Εἶτα βασίλεια, Ἀρτέμιδος ἱερὸν, Δαρείου κτίσμα, κωμόπολις· ἐνταῦθα Σεμιράμιδός ἐστι διῶρυξ, καὶ λίθοις πέφρακται ὁ Εὐφράτης, ἵνα στενοχωρούμενος ὑπερκλύζῃ τὰ πεδία· θέρους μέντοι ναυαγεῖ τὰ πλοῖα. Εἶτα Ἀλλὰν κωμόπολις, σχοῖνοι δ΄· ἔνθεν Βηονὰν, Ἀρτέμιδος ἱερὸν, σχοῖνοι δ΄. Εἶτα Φάλιγα κώμη πρὸς τῷ Εὐφράτῃ· λέγοιτο δ' ἂν ἑλληνιστὶ μεσοπορικὸν, σκοῖνοι ς΄. Ἀπὸ Ἀντιοχείας ἕως τούτου σχοῖνοι ρκ΄· ἐντεῦθεν δὲ ἐπὶ Σελεύκειαν τὴν πρὸς τῷ Τίγριδι σχοῖνοι ρ΄. Παράκειται δὲ τῇ Φάλιγα κωμόπολις Ναβαγὰθ, καὶ παραρρεῖ αὐτὴν ποταμὸς Ἀβούρας, ὅς ἐμβάλλει εἰς τὸν Εὐφράτην· ἐκεῖθεν διαβαίνει τὰ στρατόπεδα εἰς τὴν κατὰ Ῥωμαίους πέραν. Εἶτα Ἄσιχα κώμη, σχοῖνοι δ΄· ἔνθεν Δοῦρα Νικάνορος πόλις, κτίσμα Μακεδόνων, ὑπὸ δὲ Ἑλλήνων Εὔρωπος καλεῖται, σχοῖνοι ς΄. Εἶτα Μέρραν ὀχύρωμα, κωμόπολις, σχοῖνοι ε΄. Εἶτα Γιδδὰν πόλις, σχοῖνοι ε΄. Εἶτα Βηλεσὶ Βιβλάδα, σχοῖνοι ζ΄. Ἔνθεν νῆσος κατὰ τὸν Εὐφράτην, σχοῖνοι ς΄· ἐνταῦθα γάζα ἦν Φραάτου τοῦ ἀποσφάξαντος τὰς παλλακίδας, ὅτε Τηριδάτης φυγὰς ὢν εἰσέβαλεν. Εἶτα Ἀναθὼ νῆσος κατὰ τὸν Εὐφράτην σταδίων δ΄, ἐν ᾗ πόλις, σχοῖνοι δ΄· μεθ' ἣν Θιλαβοὺς νῆσος κατὰ τὸν Εὐφράτην, ἔνθα γάζα Πάρθων, σχοῖνοι β΄. Εἶτα Ἴζαν νησόπολις, σχοῖνοι ιβ΄. Εἶτα Ἀείπολις, ἔνθα ἀσφαλτίτιδες πηγαί, σχοῖνοι ις΄. Ἔνθεν Βεσήχανα πόλις, ἐν ᾗ ἱερὸν Ἀτάργατι, σχοῖνοι ιβ΄. Εἶτα Νεάπολις παρὰ τὸν Εὐφράτην, σχοῖνοι κβ΄. Ἔνθεν διαβάντων τὸν Εὐφράτην καὶ Ναρμάλχαν ἐπὶ Σελεύκειαν τὴν πρὸς τῷ Τίγριδι, σχοῖνοι θ΄. Ἄχρι τούτου Μεσοποταμία καὶ Βαβυλωνία· καὶ εἰσὶν ἀπὸ Ζεύγματος ἄχρι Σελευκείας σχοῖνοι ροα΄.

Alagma, a fortified place, a royal station, 3 schoeni; beyond which is Ichnae, a Greek city, founded by the Macedonians: it is situated on the river Balicha: 3 schoeni. Then Nicephorium by the Euphrates, a Greek city, founded by King Alexander, 5 schoeni. Farther on, by the river, is Galabatha, a deserted village, 4 schoeni. Then the village of Chumbana, 1 schoenus; farther on Thillada Mirrhada, a royal station, 4 schoeni. Then a royal place, a temple of Artemis, founded by Darius, a small town; close by is the canal of Semiramis, and the Euphrates is dammed with rocks, in order that by being thus checked it may overflow the fields; but also in summer it wrecks the boats; to this place, 7 schoeni. Then Allan, a walled village, 4 schoeni. Then Phaliga, a village on the Euphrates (that means in Greek *half-way*), 6 schoeni. From Antioch to this place, 120 schoeni; and from thence to Seleucia, which is on the Tigris, 100 schoeni. Nearby Phaliga is the walled village of Nabagath, and by it flows the river Aburas, which empties into the Euphrates; there the legions cross over to the Roman territory beyond the river. Then the village of Asich, 4 schoeni; beyond which is the city of Dura Nicanoris, founded by the Macedonians, also called by the Greeks Europus, 6 schoeni. Then Merrha, a fortified place, a walled village, 5 schoeni. Then the city of Giddan, 5 schoeni. Then Belesi Biblada, 7 schoeni. Beyond is an island in the Euphrates, 6 schoeni; there was the treasure of Phraates, who cut the throats of his concubines, when Tiridates who was exiled, invaded [the land]. Then Anatho, an island in the Euphrates, of 4 stadia, on which is a city, 4 schoeni; beyond which is Thilabus, an island in the Euphrates; there is the treasure of the Parthians, 2 schoeni. Then Izan, a city on an island, 12 schoeni. Then Aipolis, [the city of Is] where there are bituminous springs, 16 schoeni. Beyond is the city of Besechana, in which is a temple of Atargatis, 12 schoeni. Then Neapolis by the Euphrates, 22 schoeni. From that place those leaving the Euphrates and passing through Narmalchan come to Seleucia on the Tigris, 9 schoeni. To this place [extend] Mesopotamia and Babylonia; and from Zeugma to Seleucia there are 171 schoeni.

2. Ἐντεῦθεν ἄρχεται ἡ Ἀπολλωνιᾶτις, ἥτις κατέχει σχοίνους λγ'. Ἔχει δὲ κώμας, ἐν αἶς σταθμός, πόλιν δὲ Ἑλληνίδα Ἀρτέμιτα· διὰ μέσης δὲ ταύτης ῥεῖ ποταμὸς Σίλλα. Εἰσὶ δὲ εἰς αὐτὴν ἀπὸ Σελευκείας σχοῖνοι ιε'. Νῦν μέντοι ἡ πόλις καλεῖται Χαλάσαρ.

3. Ἐντεῦθεν ἡ Χαλωνῖτις, σχοῖνοι κα'· ἐν ᾗ κῶμαι ε', ἐν αἷς σταθμός, πόλις δὲ Ἑλληνὶς Χάλα, ἀπὸ τῆς Ἀπολλωνιάτιδος σχοῖνοι ιε'. Εἶτα ἀπὸ σχοίνων ε' ὄρος ὃ καλεῖται Ζάγρος, ὅπερ ὁρίζει τὴν Χαλωνῖτιν χώραν καὶ τὴν τῶν Μήδων.

4. Ἐντεῦθεν Μηδία, ἥτις κατέχει σχοίνους κβ'. Ἡ ἀρχὴ αὐτῶν ἡ χώρα Κάρινα· ἐν ᾗ κῶμαι ε', ἐν αἷς σταθμός, πόλις δὲ οὐδεμία.

5. Ἐντεῦθεν Γαμβαδηνή, ἥτις κατέχει σχοίνους λα', ἐν ᾗ κῶμαι ε', ἐν αἷς σταθμός, πόλις δὲ Βάπτανα ἐπ' ὄρους κειμένη· ἔνθα Σεμιράμιδος ἄγαλμα καὶ στήλη.

6. Ἐντεῦθεν ἡ Μηδία ἡ ἄνω, σχοῖνοι λη'· καὶ ἄρχεται εὐθὺς πόλις Κογκοβάρ· ἔνθα Ἀρτέμιδος ἱερόν, σχοῖνοι γ'. Εἶτα Βαζιγράβαν, ὅ ἐστι τελώνιον, σχοῖνοι γ'. Εἶτα εἰς Ἀδραπάναν τὰ βασίλεια τῶν ἐν Βατάνοις, ἃ Τιγράνης ὁ Ἀρμένιος καθεῖλε, σχοῖνοι δ'. Εἶτα Βάτανα, μητρόπολις Μηδίας καὶ θησαυροφυλάκιον καὶ ἱερόν, ὅπερ Ἀναΐτιδος· ἀεὶ θύουσιν· σχοῖνοι ιβ'. Εἶτα ἑξῆς τρεῖς κῶμαι, ἐν αἷς σταθμός.

7. Ἐντεῦθεν [Ῥαγιανὴ] Μηδία, σχοῖνοι [νη']. Ἐν ᾗ κῶμαι ι', πόλεις δὲ ε'. Ἀπὸ σχοίνων ζ' Ῥάγα καὶ Χάραξ, ὧν μεγίστη τῶν κατὰ τὴν Μηδίαν Ῥάγα. Εἰς δὲ τὴν Χάρακα πρῶτος βασιλεὺς Φραάτης τοὺς Μάρδους ᾤκισεν· ἔστιν ὑπὸ τὸ ὄρος, ὃ καλεῖται Κάσπιος, ἀφ' οὗ Κάσπιαι πύλαι.

8. Ἐντεῦθεν ὑπερβάντων τὰς Κασπίας πύλας ἐστὶν αὐλὼν καὶ ἡ Χοαρηνή, [σχοῖνοι ιθ'] · ἐν ᾗ Ἀπάμεια πόλις ἀπὸ σχοίνων δ'· κῶμαι δὲ δ', ἐν αἷς σταθμός.

9. Ἐντεῦθεν Κομισηνή, σχοῖνοι νη', ἐν ᾗ κῶμαι η', ἐν αἷς σταθμός· πόλις δὲ οὐκ ἔστιν.

10. Ἐντεῦθεν Ὑρκανία, σχοῖνοι ξ', ἐν ᾗ κῶμαι ια', ἐν αἷς σταθμοί.

2. From that place begins Apolloniatis, which extends 33 schoeni. It has villages, in which there are stations; and a Greek city, Artemita; through the midst of which flows the river Silla. To that place from Seleucia is 15 schoeni. But now the city is called Chalasar.

3. From that place, Chalonitis, 21 schoeni; in which there are 5 villages, in which there are stations, and a Greek city, Chala, 15 schoeni beyond Apolloniatis. Then, after 5 schoeni, a mountain which is called Zagrus, which forms the boundary between the district of Chalonitis and that of the Medes.

4. From that place, [Lower] Media, which extends 22 schoeni. The beginning is at the district of Carina; in which there are 5 villages in which there are stations, but no city.

5. From that place, Cambadene, which extends 31 schoeni, in which there are 5 villages, in which there are stations, and a city, Bagistana, situated on a mountain; there is a statue and a pillar of Semiramis.

6. From that place, Upper Media, 38 schoeni; and at 3 schoeni from the very beginning of it is the city of Concobar; there is a temple of Artemis, 3 schoeni. Then Bazigraban, which is a custom house, 3 schoeni. Thence to Adrapana, the royal residence of those who ruled in Ecbatana, and which Tigranes the Armenian destroyed, 4 schoeni. Then Ecbatana, the metropolis of Media and the treasury, and a temple, sacred to Anaitis; they sacrifice there always; 12 schoeni. And beyond that place are 3 villages in which there are stations.

7. From that place [Rhagiana] Media, [58] schoeni. In it are 10 villages, and 5 cities. After 7 schoeni are Rhaga and Charax; of which Rhaga is the greatest of the cities in Media. And in Charax the first king Phraates settled the Mardi; it is beneath a mountain, which is called Caspius, beyond which are the Caspian Gates.

8. Beyond that place, for those passing through the Caspian Gates there is a narrow valley, and the district of Choarena [19 schoeni]; in which is the city of Apamia, after 4 schoeni; and there are 4 villages in which there are stations.

9. Beyond is Comisena, 58 schoeni, in which there are 8 villages in which there are stations, but there is no city.

10. Beyond is Hyrcania, 60 schoeni, in which there are 11 villages in which there are stations.

11. Ἐντεῦθεν Ἀσταυηνὴ, σχοῖνοι ξ΄, ἐν ᾗ κῶμαι ιβ΄, ἐν αἷς σταθμοί· πόλις δὲ Ἀσαὰκ, ἐν ᾗ Ἀρσάκης πρῶτος βασιλεὺς ἀπεδείχθη· καὶ φυλάττεται ἐνταῦθα πῦρ ἀθάνατον.

12. Ἐντεῦθεν Παρθυηνὴ, σχοῖνοι κε΄, ἧς αὐλών· Παρθαύνισα ἡ πόλις ἀπὸ σχοίνων ϛ΄· ἔνθα βασιλικαὶ ταφαί· Ἕλληνες δὲ Νίσαιαν λέγουσιν. Εἶτα Γάθαρ πόλις ἀπὸ σχοίνων ϛ΄. Εἶτα Σιρὼκ πόλις ἀπὸ σχοίνων ε΄. Κώμας δὲ οὐκ ἔχει πλὴν μιᾶς, ἥτις καλεῖται Σαφρί.

13. Ἐντεῦθεν Ἀπαυαρκτικηνὴ, σχοῖνοι κζ΄· ἐν ᾗ πόλις Ἀπαυαρκτική. Εἶτα Ῥαγαῦ πόλις καὶ κῶμαι δύο.

14. Ἐντεῦθεν Μαργιανὴ, σχοῖνοι λ΄. Ἔνθα Ἀντιόχεια ἡ καλουμένη Ἔνυδρος· κῶμαι δὲ οὐκ εἰσίν.

15. Ἐντεῦθεν Ἄρεια, σχοῖνοι λ΄. Ἔνθα Κανδὰκ πόλις καὶ Ἀρτακαύαν πόλις καὶ Ἀλεξάνδρεια ἡ ἐν Ἀρείοις· κῶμαι δὲ δ΄.

16. Ἐντεῦθεν Ἀναύων χώρα τῆς Ἀρείας, σχοῖνοι νε΄, ἐν ᾗ πόλις μεγίστη Φρὰ καὶ Βὶς πόλις καὶ Γαρὶ πόλις καὶ Νιὴ πόλις· κώμη δὲ οὐκ ἔστιν.

17. Ἐντεῦθεν Ζαραγγιανὴ, σχοῖνοι κα΄. Ἔνθα πόλις Πάριν καὶ Κορὸκ πόλις.

18. Ἐντεῦθεν Σακαστανὴ Σακῶν Σκυθῶν, ἡ καὶ Παραιτακηνὴ, σχοῖνοι ξγ΄. Ἔνθα Βαρδὰ πόλις καὶ Μὶν πόλις καὶ Παλακεντὶ πόλις καὶ Σιγὰλ πόλις· ἔνθα βασίλεια Σακῶν· καὶ πλησίον Ἀλεξάνδρεια πόλις (καὶ πλησίον Ἀλεξανδρόπολις πόλις)· κῶμαι δὲ ἔξ.

19. Ἐντεῦθεν Ἀραχωσία, σχοῖνοι λϛ΄. Ταύτην δὲ οἱ Πάρθοι Ἰνδικὴν Λευκὴν καλοῦσιν· ἔνθα Βιὺτ πόλις καὶ Φάρσανα πόλις καὶ Χοροχοὰδ πόλις καὶ Δημητριὰς πόλις· εἶτα Ἀλεξανδρόπολις, μητρόπολις Ἀραχωσίας· ἔστι δὲ Ἑλληνίς, καὶ παραρρεῖ αὐτὴν ποταμὸς Ἀραχωτός. Ἄχρι τούτου ἐστὶν ἡ τῶν Πάρθων ἐπικράτεια.

Ἰσιδώρου Χαρακηνοῦ σταθμοὶ Παρθικοι.

11. Beyond is Astauena, 60 schoeni, in which there are 12 villages in which there are stations; and the city of Asaac, in which Arsaces was first proclaimed king; and an everlasting fire is guarded there.

12. Beyond is Parthyena, 25 schoeni; within which is a valley, and the city of Parthaunisa after 6 schoeni; there are royal tombs. But the Greeks call it Nisaea. Then the city of Gathar after 6 schoeni. Then the city of Siroc after 5 schoeni. Of villages it has no more than one, which is called Saphri.

13. Beyond is Apauarcticena, 27 schoeni, in which is the city of Apauarctica. Then the city of Ragau and two villages.

14. Beyond is Margiana, 30 schoeni. There is Antiochia, called *well-watered;* but there are no villages.

15. Beyond is Aria, 30 schoeni. There are the city of Candac and the city of Artacauan and Alexandria of the Arii; and 4 villages.

16. Beyond is Anauon, a region of Aria, 55 schoeni, in which is a very great city, Phra, and the city of Bis, and the city of Gari and the city of Nia; but there is no village.

17. Beyond is Zarangiana, 21 schoeni. There are the city of Parin and the city of Coroc.

18. Beyond is Sacastana of the Scythian Sacae, which is also Paraetacena, 63 schoeni. There are the city of Barda and the city of Min and the city of Palacenti and the city of Sigal; in that place is the royal residence of the Sacae; and nearby is the city of Alexandria (and nearby is the city of Alexandropolis), and 6 villages.

19. Beyond is Arachosia, 36 schoeni. And the Parthians call this White India; there are the city of Biyt and the city of Pharsana and the city of Chorochoad and the city of Demetrias; then Alexandropolis, the metropolis of Arachosia; it is Greek, and by it flows the river Arachotus. As far as this place the land is under the rule of the Parthians.

The Parthian Stations of Isidore of Charax.

ΠΑΡΘΙΑΣ ΠΕΡΙΗΓΗΣΙΣ

20. Athenæus III, p 93, D: Ἰσίδωρος δ' ὁ Χαρακηνὸς ἐν τῷ τῆς Παρθίας Περιηγητικῷ κατὰ τὸ Περσικὸν πέλαγος νῆσόν φησιν εἶναί τινα, ἔνθα πλείστην μαργαρῖτιν εὑρίσκεσθαι. Διόπερ σχεδίας καλαμίνας πέριξ εἶναι τῆς νήσου, ἐξ ὧν καθαλλομένους εἰς τὴν θάλασσαν ἐπ' ὀργυιὰς εἴκοσιν ἀναφέρειν διπλοῦς κόγκους. Φασὶ δ', ὅταν βρονταὶ συνεχεῖς ὦσι καὶ ὄμβρων ἐκχύσεις, τότε μᾶλλον τὴν πίνναν κύειν, καὶ πλείστην γίγνεσθαι μαργαρῖτιν καὶ εὐμεγέθη. Τοῦ δὲ χειμῶνος εἰς τὰς ἐμβυθίους θαλάμας δύνειν εἰώθασιν αἱ πίνναι· θέρους δὲ τὰς μὲν νύκτας κεχήνασι διανηχόμεναι, ἡμέρας δὲ μύουσιν. Ὅσαι δ' ἂν πέτραις ἢ σπιλάσι προσφυῶσι, ῥιζοβολοῦσι, κἀνταῦθα ἐνδῦσαι τὴν μαργαρῖτιν γεννῶσι. Ζωογονοῦνται δὲ καὶ τρέφονται διὰ τοῦ προσπεφυκότος τῇ σαρκὶ μέρους. Τοῦτο δὲ συμπέφυκε τῷ τοῦ κόγχου στόματι, χηλὰς ἔχον καὶ νομὴν εἰσφέρον. Ὃ δή ἐστιν ἐοικὸς καρκίνῳ μικρῷ, καλούμενον πιννοφύλαξ. Διήκει δ' ἐκ τούτου ἡ σὰρξ μέχρι μέσου τοῦ κόγχου, οἱονεὶ ῥίζα, παρ' ἣν ἡ μαργαρῖτις γεννωμένη, αὔξεται διὰ τοῦ στερεοῦ τῆς κόγχης, καὶ τρέφεται, ὅσον ἂν ᾖ προσπεφυκυῖα χρόνον. Ἐπειδὰν δὲ παρὰ τὴν ἔκφυσιν ὑποδυομένη ἡ σὰρξ καὶ μαλακῶς ἐντέμνουσα χωρίσῃ τὴν μαργαρῖτιν ἀπὸ τοῦ κόγχου, ἀμπέχουσα μὲν οὐκέτι τρέφει, λειοτέραν δ' αὐτὴν καὶ διαυγεστέραν ποιεῖ καὶ καθαρωτέραν. Ἡ μὲν οὖν ἐμβύθιος πίννα διαυγεστάτην ποιεῖ καὶ καθαρωτάτην καὶ μεγάλην γεννᾷ μαργαρῖτιν, ἡ δὲ ἐπιπολάζουσα καὶ ἀνωφερὴς διὰ τὸ ὑπὸ τοῦ ἡλίου ἀκτινοβολεῖσθαι, δύσχρους καὶ ἥσσων. Κινδυνεύουσι δ' οἱ θηρῶντες τοὺς μαργαρίτας, ὅταν εἰς κεχηνότα κόγχον κατ' εὐθὺ ἐκτείνωσι τὴν χεῖρα· μύει γὰρ τότε, καὶ πολλάκις οἱ δάκτυλοι αὐτῶν ἀποπρίονται· ἔνιοι δὲ καὶ παραχρῆμα ἀποθνήσκουσιν. Ὅσοι δ' ἂν ἐκ πλαγίου ὑποθέντες τὴν χεῖρα τύχωσι, ῥᾳδίως τοὺς κόγχους ἀπὸ τοῦ λίθου ἀποσπῶσιν.

JOURNEY AROUND PARTHIA

20. (A fragment quoted from Athenæus, III, 46.) Isidore of Charax in his description of Parthia says there is a certain island in the Persian Gulf where many pearls are found; and that round about the island there are rafts made of reeds, from which men dive into the sea to a depth of 20 fathoms and bring up double-shelled oysters. They say that when there are frequent thunderstorms and heavy rains, the oyster produces the most young, and they get the most, the best and the largest pearls; and in the winter the shells are accustomed to sink into holes in the bottom, but in the summer they swim about all night with their shells open, but they close in the daytime. And when they cling to stones and rocks in the waves they take root and then, remaining fixed, produce the pearls. These are engendered and nourished by something that adheres to their flesh. It grows in the mouth of the oyster and has claws and brings in food. It is like a small crab and is called "Guardian of the oyster." Its flesh penetrates through the center of the shell like a root; the pearl being engendered close to it, grows through the solid portion of the shell and keeps growing as long as it continues to adhere to the shell. But when the flesh gets under the excrescence and cuts its way onward, it gently separates the pearl from the shell and then, when the pearl is surrounded by flesh, it is no longer nourished in such manner as to grow further, but the flesh makes it smoother, more transparent and more pure. And when the oyster lives at the bottom, it produces the clearest and largest pearls; but those that float on the surface, because they are affected by the rays of the sun, produce smaller pearls, of poorer color. The pearl divers run into danger when they thrust their hands straight into the open oyster, for it closes up and their fingers are often cut off, and sometimes they perish on the spot; but those who take them by thrusting their hands under from one side, easily pull the shells off from the rocks.

[ISIDORI ORBIS TERRARUM DESCRIPTIO]

21. Plinius *Hist. Nat.*, *II*, *112 :* Pars nostra terrarum, de qua memoro, ambienti oceano velut innatans longissime ab ortu ad occasum patet, hoc est ab India ad Herculis columnas Gadibus sacratas $\overline{\text{LXXXV}}$. LXVIII mill. pass., ut Artemidoro auctori placet, ut vero Isidoro, $\overline{\text{XCVIII}}$. et XVIII. M.

22. *Id. II*, *112 :* Latitudo autem terrae a meridiano situ ad septentriones dimidio fere minor colligitur $\overline{\text{XLIIII}}$. LXXXX milia. *Sequuntur partes hujus mensurae quae pertinent a meridie ultima usque ad ostum Tanais* (*V fr. Artemid.*) *Dein Plinius pergit:* Ab ostio Tanais nihil modi quam diligentissimi auctores fecere; Artemidorus ulteriora incomperta existumavit, quum circa Tanaim Sarmatarum gentis degere fateretur ad septentriones versus; Isidorus adjecit duodeciens centena millia quinquaginta usque ad Thulen, quœ conjectura divinationes est.

23. *Id. V. 9 :* Universam vero (*Asiam*) cum Ægypto ad Tanaim Artemidorus et Isidorus $\overline{\text{LXIII}}$ LXXV M. p. (esse tradunt).

24. *Id. IV. 37 :* Longitudinem ejus (*Europae*) Artemidorus atque Isidorus a Tanai Gadis $\overline{\text{LXXXII}}$ XIIII M. p. prodiderunt.

25. *Id. V. 6 :* Isidorus a Tingi Canopum $\overline{\text{XXXV}}$. XCIX M. p., Artemidorus XL M̂. minus quam Isidorus (esse existumant).

26. *Id. V. 43 :* A Chalcedone Sigeum Isidorus CCCXXII (CCCXII et CCCLXII v. 1.) M. D. p. tradit.

27. *Id. V. 35 :* Hujus (*Cypri*) circuitum Timosthenes CCCCXXVII M. D. prodidit, Isidorus CCCLXXV.

28. *Id. V. 36 :* Distat (*Rhodus*) ab Alexandria Ægypti DLXXXIII M, ut Isidorus tradit; ut Eratosthenes, CCCCLXIX M; ut Mucianus, D, a Cypro CLXVI.

FROM ISIDORE'S DESCRIPTION OF THE WORLD

21. (Pliny, *Natural History*, II, 112.) "Our part of the earth, of which I propose to give an account, floating as it were in the ocean which surrounds it, stretches out to the greatest extent from east to west, viz., from India to the Pillars consecrated to Hercules at Gades, being a distance of 8568 miles, according to the statement of Artemidorus, or according to that of Isidore, 9818 miles."

22. (*Ibid.*, II, 112.) "The breadth of the earth from south to north, is commonly supposed to be about one-half only of its length, viz., 4490 miles;" (then follow parts of these measurements from the southern extremities to the mouth of Tanais). "Beyond the Tanais the most diligent authors have not been able to obtain any accurate measurement. Artemidorus supposes that everything beyond is undiscovered, since he confesses that, about the Tanais, the tribes of the Sarmatae dwell, who extend toward the North Pole. Isidore adds 1250 miles, as the distance to Thule; but this is mere conjecture."

23. (*Ibid.*, V, 9.) "The whole distance (of Asia) to the Tanais, including Egypt, is, according to Artemidorus and Isidore, 6375 miles.

24. (*Ibid.*, IV, 37.) "Artemidorus and Isidore have given the length of it (Europe) from the Tanais to Gades, as 8214 miles."

25. (*Ibid.*, V, 6.) "Isidore speaks of the distance from Tingi to Canopus as being 3599 miles. Artemidorus makes this last distance forty miles less than Isidore."

26. (*Ibid.* V, 43.) "From Chalcedon to Sigeum, Isidore makes the distance 322½ miles."

27. (*Ibid.*, V, 35.) "Timosthenes states that the circumference of this island [Cyprus] is 427 miles, Isidore 375."

28. (*Ibid.*, V, 36.) "The fairest of them all is the free island of Rhodes, 125, or if we would rather believe Isidore, 103 miles in circumference . . . . It is distant from Alexandria in Egypt, according to Isidore, 583 miles; but according to Eratosthenes, 469. Mucianus says that its distance from Cyprus is 166."

29. *Id. V. 37 :* Ioniæ ora habet...Samon liberam circuitu LXXXVII. M D. p., aut, ut Isidorus, C M.

30. *Id. V. 38 :* (*Chius insula*) circuitu CXXV M. p. colligit, ut veteres tradidere, Isidorus IX M. adicit.

31. *Id. V. 39 :* Tota insula (*Lesbus*) circuitur, ut Isidorus, CLXVIII M. p., ut veteres, CXCV M.

32. *Id. IV. 5 :* Peloponnesus.. inter duo maria, Ægæum et Ionium, platani folio similis, propter angulosos recessus circuitu DLXIII M. p. colligit, auctore Isidoro. Eadem per sinus pæne tantundem adicit.

33. *Id. IV. 30 :* Hæc (*Britannia*) abest a Gesoriaco Morinorum gentis litore proximo trajectu L M : circuitu patere $\overline{XXXXVIII}$· LXXV M. Pytheas et Isidorus tradunt.

EX ISIDORI CHARACENI OPERA INCERTO

34. Lucianus Macrob. c. 15 : Ἀρταξέρξης ἕτερος Περσῶν βασιλεὺς, ὅν φησιν ἐπὶ τῶν πατέρων ἑαυτοῦ Ἰσίδωρος ὁ Χαρακηνὸς συγγραφεὺς βασιλεύειν, ἔτη τρία καὶ ἐνενήκοντα βιοὺς ἐπιβουλῇ τἀδελφοῦ Γωσίθρου ἐδολοφονήθη.

35. Id. ib. c. 18 : Γόαισος δὲ, ὥς φησιν Ἰσίδωρος ὁ Χαρακηνὸς, ἐπὶ τῆς ἑαυτοῦ ἡλικίας Ὀμανῶν τῆς ἀρωματοφόρου βασιλεύσας πεντεκαίδεκα καὶ ἑκατὸν γεγονὼς ἐτῶν ἐτελεύτησε νόσῳ.

29. (*Ibid.*, V, 37.) "The coast of Ionia has ......
Samos, a free island, eighty-seven miles in circumference, or, according to Isidore, 100."

30. (*Ibid.*, V, 38.) "The free island of Chios......
is 125 miles in circumference, according to the ancient writers; Isidore, however, makes it nine more."

31. (*Ibid.*, V, 39.) "The circumference of the whole island [Lesbos] is, according to Isidore, 168 miles; but the older writers say 195."

32. (*Ibid.*, IV, 5.) "The Peloponnesus, ... situate between two seas, the Aegean and the Ionian, is in shape like the leaf of a plane-tree, in consequence of the angular indentations made in its shores. According to Isidore, it is 563 miles in circumference; and nearly as much again, allowing for the coast-line on the shores of its bays."

33. (*Ibid.*, IV, 30.) "This island [Britain] is distant from Gesoriacum, on the coast of the nation of the Morini, at the spot where the passage across is shortest, fifty miles. Pytheas and Isidore say that its circumference is 4875 miles."

FROM AN UNKNOWN WORK BY ISIDORE OF CHARAX

34. (Fragment quoted from Lucianus, *Macrob.* ch. 15.) "Artaxerxes, another king of the Persians, whom Isidore of Charax the historian states to have ruled in the time of his parents, after a life of ninety-three years, was treacherously murdered through a plot of his brother Gosithras."

35. (Id. *ib.* ch. 18:) "Goaesus, so says Isidore of Charax, who in his time was king of the Omani in the Incense Land, after he had lived one hundred and fifteen years, died of disease."

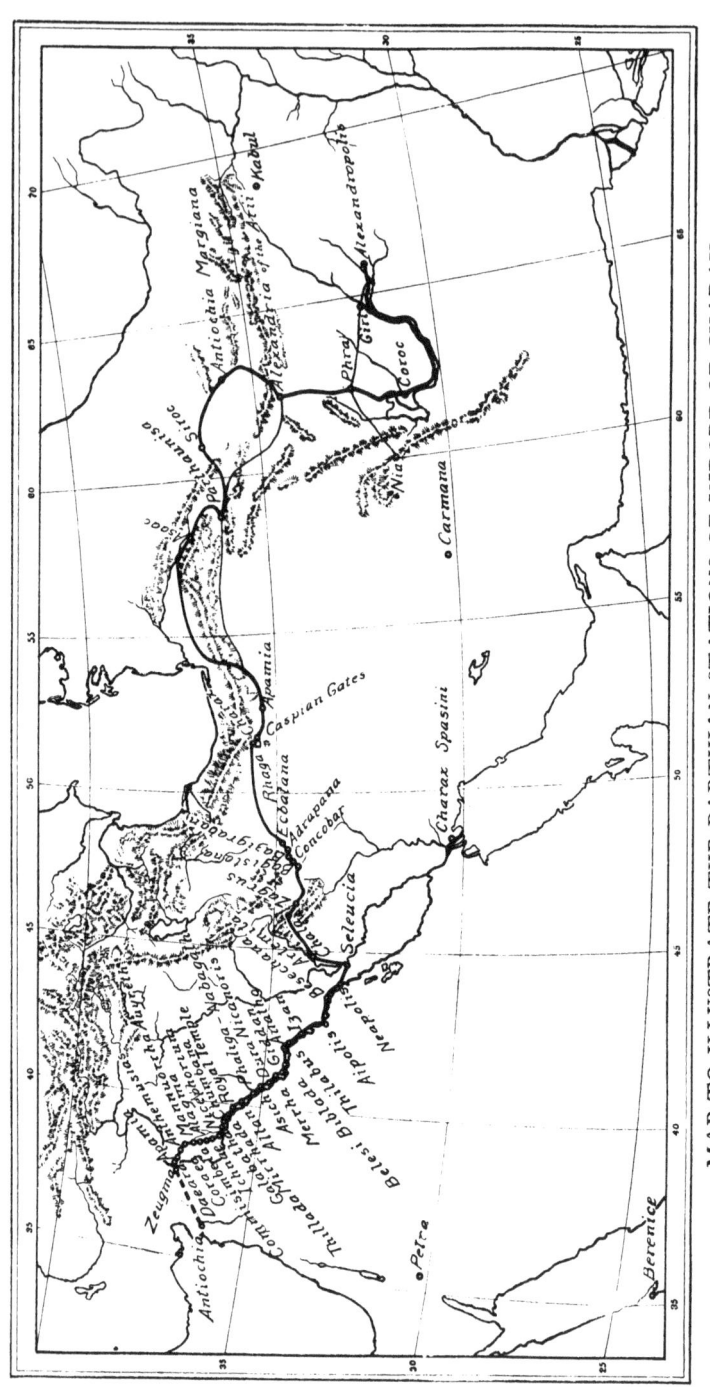

MAP TO ILLUSTRATE THE PARTHIAN STATIONS OF ISIDORE OF CHARAX

COMMENTARY

The *Parthian Stations* of Isidore of Charax, fragmentary as it is, is one of the very few records of the overland trade-route in the period of struggle between Parthia and Rome. As the title indicates, it gives an itinerary of the caravan trail from Antioch to the borders of India, naming the supply stations, or, as they would now be called, the caravanserais maintained by the Parthian Government for the convenience of merchants. While the record contains little more than the names of the stations and the intervening distances, an examination of the route followed leads to numerous inferences concerning the relations of the Parthian monarchy with its subject states and with neighboring foreign powers.

This record may be dated from internal evidence as of the reign of Augustus, probably very close to the Christian era. In its manuscript form, the *Parthian Stations* seems to be a mere summary or transcription from some larger work, and another extract quoted by Athenaeus and ascribed to Isidore, mentions the title as a "Journey around Parthia," while various fragments quoted in the *Natural History* of Pliny indicate that Isidore was the author of some general work on geography. His very home is a matter of inference. The manuscript speaks of him as Isidore "of Charax," which means merely "palisaded town." But it seems clear that the place meant is Charax Spasini, the commercial port at the head of the Persian Gulf, and C. Müller points out that the author of the "description of the world" mentioned by Pliny (VI, 31) as having been commissioned by Augustus "to gather all necessary information in the east when his eldest son was about to set out for Armenia to take the command against the Parthians and Arabians," is no other than our Isidore. The manuscript of Pliny in that place refers this work to Dionysius, but as both Müller and Bernhardy have shown, this is a mistake and Isidore is probably meant.

As to the date of the work of Isidore, as it mentions the second revolution of Tiridates against the Parthian king Phraates, which took place in 26 B. C., it must be later than that date; and a subsequent reference to a king named Goaesus of the "Incense Land" in South Arabia, while his dates are not definitely known, suggests as Glaser has shown, a time very near the Christian era.

The route followed in the *Parthian Stations* beginning at Antioch, crosses the Euphrates at Zeugma, the modern Birijik. This was on the high-road to Edessa and Armenia. After crossing the Euphrates the Parthian route made a direct line, avoiding the long bend in the river, which it reached lower down and followed until Neapolis, where it left the Euphrates and crossed overland to Seleucia on the Tigris. Thence it ascended the hills of Media, crossed the Caspian Gates, and followed the fertile valleys eastward through the modern Khorassan to the Herat river. Here, instead of proceeding eastward to Bactria and the Pamirs, the Parthian route turned southward to Lake Helmund and Kandahar, where the record ends.

If the route laid down in the *Parthian Stations* was the high-road of commerce under the Parthian Empire, it suggests not only a thorough regulation of commerce throughout its own dominions, but also a lack of trade control in other states generally counted as tributary to the Parthians, who evidently attended to their own commercial affairs. Isidore speaks of the two revolts against Phraates who, we are told by various Roman historians, was expelled from the capital and forced to flee to the Scythians, by whom he was given aid, returned and reestablished himself on his throne. The Scythian king is not named, but he probably ruled over the Saka Scythians, who had been driven westward from Chinese territory by the Yue-chi, who had set up in the former Greek kingdom of Bactria a powerful kingdom under the Kushan dynasty some fifty years before Isidore's time. The Saka tribes had migrated ahead of the Yue-chi and had settled in the Helmund valley, acknowledging some sort of dependence upon the Parthian dynasty. In Indian history we find the Indo-Parthians overrunning the Cambay district in the first century A. D. and a combination known in Indian records as Sakas, Yavanas and Pallavas, raiding much farther south in the two centuries following. These are no doubt the same tribes that lent aid to Phraates against his rebellious subjects. The subservience of the Saka Scythians to the Parthian dynasty must have been little more than nominal. Their chieftains in India acknowledged the over-lordship of the Kushan monarchies and they seem to have been free lances. In matters commercial we may infer that they not only served as the eastern terminus of the Parthian trade route, but that they cooperated with the Kushan kings in maintaining trade relations through Carmania and Persia with the Arab states of Mesene and Characene at the head of the Persian Gulf. Along this route a trade in Chinese silks was carried on between the Pamirs and Charax Spasini, whence the merchandise went by sailing vessels around Arabia, and finally reached the Levant through the mart of Petra. Such trade as passed through Parthia and came directly under the control of the Parthian monarchy went over the route sketched by Isidore, ending at Antioch; and it is interesting to note that the Parthian route includes the space between Kandahar and Lake Helmund, which had also to be traveled by those bound for the Persian Gulf. It is clear that the southern kingdoms tributary to the Parthian state were in large measure independent in their commercial affairs, and that some understanding to this effect existed with the Parthian capital; otherwise the diversion of trade between the northern and southern routes at Lake Helmund could not peacefully have occurred.*

The *Parthian Stations* marks the ancient trade-route of the Medes and the Assyrians. The rise of the power of Persia diverted much of the trade to the Royal Road, leading to Susa and thence to Lake Helmund. Under the Parthians it was evidently a state policy to encourage the passage of goods from Lake Helmund over the old northern route; but the understanding between the Kushan monarchy and the Nabatæan princes made it impracticable for Parthia to establish a commercial monopoly through its capital on the Tigris.

We may infer that the author of the *Journey Around Parthia*, meaning the Parthian Empire, described both these important overland highways. It is very regrettable that his work should have perished except in fugitive quotations, and that we have remaining only a brief itinerary of the northern route.

The policy of the Roman Empire during the two centuries following the Christian era was to encourage direct sea trade with India, cutting out all overland routes through Parthia and thus avoiding the annoyance of fiscal dependence on that consistent enemy of Rome.

In connection with the work of Isidore, the relations between Parthia and Rome immediately preceding his time may be borne in mind. When Crassus became consul in Rome in 55 B. C., he was appointed to command in the east, his headquarters being at Antioch, the former Seleucid capital; and he announced his intention of carrying the Roman arms to Bactria, India and the eastern ocean. The Arab sheikhs bordering on the province of Syria, some of whom had been allied with Rome, changed sides as they did not desire further aggressions from the west. Crassus crossed the Euphrates at Zeugma, where the *Parthian Stations* begins its account. Instead of following the road to Edessa and Armenia at the foot of the hills or keeping close to the Euphrates river, he marched straight overland, still along

---

*In the *Shah Nama* the contempt of Persia for the Parthians is evident; "the throne did not belong to any one" and "men said that they had no longer a kingdom on the earth".

the route of Isidore, and was disastrously defeated at Carrhæ (Harran) half his army being killed and a quarter of his men being captured and transported by the Parthians to the distant oasis of Merv. The advantage gained by the Parthians was followed up in 51 B. C. by an invasion of Syria under Pacorus, son of the Parthian king Orodes, in which the Roman arms were all but driven from the eastern Mediterranean. The Parthians failed to establish themselves in the invaded territory and retired the next year. Again in 40 B. C. during the Roman civil war, the Parthians attacked Syria, subdued Antioch and invaded Phœnicia, Palestine and Asia Minor. After a strenuous campaign directed by Mark Antony, his general Ventidius inflicted a great defeat on the Parthians in a battle at the Euphrates, in which Pacorus was killed. At this juncture Orodes, the Parthian king, abdicated in favor of one of his sons Phraates IV, (the same mentioned by Isidore) by whom he was soon murdered. Mark Antony then invaded Parthia with an army of about 100,000 men, this being in 37 B. C. His crossing of the Euphrates being opposed in strength, he turned into Armenia and carried on a year's campaign in upper Media, from which he was compelled to retire. Phraates then invaded Media and expelled the Romans, returning to his capital in triumph, where his cruelty and excesses led to a revolt of his subjects in 33 B. C. Phraates was compelled to quit the country and Tiridates was proclaimed king by the insurgents. Phraates soon returned, however, with an army supplied by his Scythian allies, and drove out Tiridates, who fled from the Parthian dominions and surrendered in Syria to Octavian, later the Emperor Augustus, who was then, 30 B. C., in Syria on his return from Egypt. Tiridates took with him as hostage a young son of Phraates whom he had kidnapped. Octavian returned the young prince but kept Tiridates in Syria under pension, his policy being to control this very useful pretender to the Parthian throne. Once again, in 26 B. C., Tiridates invaded Parthian territory and established himself under the title of Arsaces Philoromaeus. Some coins of that year bearing his superscription may be found in modern collections. His second assumption of power lasted only a few months, when he was once more expelled and joined Augustus in Spain.

In 20 B. C., after long negotiations with Augustus, Phraates IV restored the Roman standards captured from Crassus 35 years before, and the peace so established was not seriously disturbed until Trajan's invasion of the Parthian dominion in the second century A. D. A few minor differences, it is true, over Armenian affairs led to campaigns between Rome and Parthia during the first century, but without marked effect on boundaries or trade relations. The warfare between 55 and 20 B. C. had left the two empires with a wholesome respect for each other; and Augustus left it as a principle of imperial policy that the west bank of the Euphrates was the proper limit for the Roman Empire, beyond which the power of Rome could not with advantage be extended.

The following manuscripts contain the text of Isidore:

Codex Parisinus 443, (Suppl. p 106, 2-111, 9)
" Vaticanus (fol. 236 R.-238 R. lin. 12)
" Monacensis (fol. 50 sq.)
" Parisinus 571, fol. 417 R.-418

Printed editions of Isidore of Charax have been as follows:

Hoeschelius	1600
Hudson (Oxford)	1703
Zosimiadon (Vienna)	1806
Fabricius (Dresden)	1849
Müller (Paris)	1853

The text followed in the present edition is that of C. Müller in his *Geographi Græci Minores*, Paris 1853, vol. I. pp. 244-256.

A CAMEL CARAVAN WAITING TO FORD THE RIVER

NOTES

SUMMARY. The SCHOENUS or Parasang was a Persian measure, perhaps not altogether fixed, and may be calculated as somewhere between 3¼ and 3½ miles; more or less, perhaps, an hour's travel by caravan. According to Strabo, it was equal to 40 stadia, but varied from 30 to 60.

(Strabo XV, I, II.) "When I ascended the hills, the measures of these schoeni were not everywhere uniform, so that the same number sometimes designated a greater, sometimes a less actual extent of road, a variation which dates from the earliest time and exists in our days."

Masson notes Isidore's schoenus in Persia was about 2½ miles; on the Euphrates, 3¼. Cf. Herodotus I, 66.

The STATHMOS was also a measure of distance, but irregular, depending on the nature of the country and the capability of the beasts of burden.

Athenæus (XI, 103) speaks of Amyntas as the author of a work on the Stations of Asia; Eratosthenes based some of his geographical calculations on the "Register of the Stathmi."

The modern FARSAKH in Persia is approximately the same, 3½ to 4 miles.

In general the route followed in Isidore's itinerary is from Antioch to Birijik, thence down the Euphrates to Hit and across to Seleucia on the Tigris, a short distance below Bagdad; thence by the modern caravan route from Bagdad to Hamadan, Teheran and Nishapur, thence southward to Herat and Lake Helmund, and eastward to Kandahar.

§ I. ZEUGMA and APAMIA (not to be confused with the Zeugma by Thapsacus where Alexander crossed the river; cf. Strabo, XVI, 1, 23. Zeugma means simply ford, or crossing).

This is mentioned by Pliny, V, 21; "Zeugma, 72 miles from Samosata, a fine crossing of the Euphrates. Seleucus Nicator joined it to Apamia on the opposite bank by a bridge."

Strabo mentions not Apamia, but Seleucia as opposite Zeugma (XVI, 2, 3); so Polybius V, 43, 1.

Stephanus Byz. speaks of "Seleucus by Apamia in Syria."

Pliny (VI, 30), speaks of Apamia alone.

Whether two places or two names for the same place is not known.

This crossing is at the modern Birijik (37° N., 38° E.)

§ I. DAEARA: in the Peutinger Tables this is Thiar.

§ I. ANTHEMUSIAS; see also Tacitus, Ann. VI, 41; Pliny, V, 21; Steph. Byz.

§ I. BELECHA, or BALICHA: this is the modern Belikh or Balikh, flowing from north to south, and joining the Euphrates below Rakka.

§ I. ICHNAE: see also Plutarch, *Crassus* 25, Dio Cassius XL, 12.

§ I. NICEPHORIUM: a Greek city, founded by Alexander, (or according to Appian, *Syr.* 57 by Seleucus Nicator) near the junction of the Balikh with the Euphrates: the modern Rakka (35° 50' N., 39° 5' E.) cf. Pliny, V, 21; V, 30; Strabo, (XVI, 1, 2, 3) Dio Cassius CL, 13. Later it was known as Callinicum; cf. Ammianus Marcellinus XXIII, 3.

§ I. THILLADA MIRRHADA, perhaps the modern Khmeida.

§ I. ROYAL PALACE AND SHRINE, perhaps Zelebiyeh, opposite the fortress of Zenobia, (Halebiyeh), a castle 315 feet high.

§ I. CANAL OF SEMIRAMIS: this was an irrigation ditch; Chesney reported traces of such a canal below Zelebiyeh.

It was at no great distance from this point on Isidore's itinerary that the great defeat of the Roman army under Crassus by the Parthians took place in B. C. 53.

§ I. PHALIGA and NABAGATH: these are practically identical with the Roman Circesium, the Arab Karkisiya, the modern Buseira. (35° 8'N., 40° 25'E.)

§ I. ABURAS RIVER: the modern Khabur. cf. Pliny XXXI, 22, XXXII, 7. (Chabura); Ptolemy, (Chaboras); Ezekiel, I, 1. (Chabor); Idrisi (El Chabur); Abulfeda (El Chaburi). In the Peutinger tables, Fons Scabore, Xenophon, Araxes. Under Diocletian, Circesium by the Chabura was made the frontier station of the the Roman Empire. It was captured by Chosroes and repaired by Justinian.

§ I. ASICH, the Zeitha of Ptolemy and Ammianus Marcellinus. Perhaps the mounds of Jemma. cf. Ammianus Marcellinus, XXIII, 5; "here we saw the tomb of the emperor Gordian, which is visible for a long way off." It still shows a wall and ditch, enclosing numerous ruins.

§ I. DURA NICANORIS, perhaps the Theltha of Ptolemy, the modern Tel Abu'l Hassan.

§ I. MERRHA or MERRHAN, the modern Irzi; very near to the Corsote of Xenophon, where Cyrus provisioned his army; and where the Emperor Julian stopped to hunt wild deer for his forces.

§ I. GIDDAN is perhaps the modern Jabariyeh. The island station is uncertain, there being numerous islands in this part of the river; perhaps Karabileh, said to show ruins.

§ I. ANATHO is the modern 'Ana (34° 25' N., 42° E.) which is on the bank of the river, whereas the Anatho of Isidore was on an island, evidently Lubbad just below 'Ana, where there is a ruined fortress; c. f. Ammianus Marcellinus, XXIV. Formerly the island was connected with both banks by bridges.

§ I. THILABUS or Olabus; perhaps the modern Haditha.

§ I. IZAN or Izannesopolis, possibly the island El Uzz.

§ I. AIPOLIS, the modern Hit (33° 26' N., 42° 48' E.). Here are the bituminous springs, often referred to by Greek and Roman writers; cf. Herodotus I, 179.

§ I. PHRAATES (Phraates IV, 37 B. C.) Parthian King, son of Orodes I. Murdered his father and all his thirty brothers

A Tetradrachm of Phraates IV in the British Museum

Same Coin Redrawn

(Justin XLII, 5; Plut. *Crass* 33; Dio Cass. XLIX, 33). Attacked by Mark Antony in 36 B. C. he repulsed the Romans; invaded

Armenia and Atropatene and gained territory from Augustus. His many cruelties led to the revolt of the Parthians under Tiridates in 32 B. C., only put down by help of the Scythians. In 20 B. C. returned the Roman eagles captured from Crassus; acknowledged Roman supremacy in Armenia, and sent five sons as hostages to Augustus, under advice of an Italian concubine whom he married under name of "Goddess Musa"; her son, Phraates V, or Phraataces, he appointed his successor. Was murdered by Musa and Phraataces, 4 B. C. (Josephus, *Ant.* XVIII, 2, 4; *Encycl. Brit.* XXI, 533.)

§ I. TIRIDATES (sometimes called Tiridates II) was set up by the Parthians in 32 B. C. against Phraates IV, but expelled when Phraates returned with the help of the Scythians. (Dio Cass. LI, 18; Justin XLIII, 5; cf. Horace, Od. I, 26.) Tiridates fled to Syria, where Augustus allowed him to stay, but refused to support him. He invaded Parthia again; coins of 26 B. C. were issued by

A Tetradrachm of Tiridates II in the British Museum

Same Coin Redrawn, showing title *Philoromaios* in addition to the customary *Philellenos*

him under the title of "Arsakes Philoromaios." Once more expelled, he took a son of Phraates to Augustus in Spain. The boy was returned, but Augustus refused to surrender "the fugitive slave Tiridates" (Justin XLIII, 5; Dio LIII, 33; *Encycl. Brit.* XXVI, 1010), whom he kept under pension in Syria as an ever-useful pretender to the Parthian throne in case Phraates should again become troublesome. Cf. W. Wroth, *Catalogue of the Coins of Parthia in the British Museum*, XXXVIII, and plate XXIII.

§ I. SELEUCIA on the Tigris.

Strabo says: "In former times the capital of Assyria was Babylon; it is now called Seleucia upon the Tigris. Near it is a large village called Ctesiphon. This the Parthian kings usually made their winter residence, with a view to sparing the Seleucians the burden of furnishing quarters for the Scythian soldiery. In consequence of the power of Parthia, Ctesiphon may be considered as a city rather than a village; from its size it is capable of lodging a great multitude of people; it has been adorned with public buildings by the Parthians and has furnished merchandise and given rise to arts profitable to its masters. The kings usually passed the winter there, on account of the salubrity of the air, and the summer at Ecbatana and in Hyrcania, induced by the ancient renown of these places. (XXI, I, 16.)

"Babylon .... is situated in a plain ..... The tomb of Belus is there. At present it is in ruins, having been demolished, as it is said, by Xerxes ..... Alexander intended to repair it. It was a great undertaking ..... so that he was not able to execute what he had attempted, before disease hurried him rapidly to his end. None of the persons who succeeded him attended to this undertaking; other works also were neglected, and the city was dilapidated, partly by the Persians, partly by time, and through the indifference of the Macedonians to things of this kind, particularly after Seleucus Nicator had fortified Seleucia on the Tigris near Babylon, at the distance of about 300 stadia.

"Both this prince and all his successors directed their care to that city, and transferred to it the seat of empire. At present it is larger than Babylon, which is in great part deserted. . . . .

"On account of the scarcity of timber, the beams and pillars of the houses are made of palm wood. They wind ropes of twisted reed round the pillars, paint them over with colors and draw designs upon them; they cover the doors with a coat of asphaltum. These are lofty and all the houses are vaulted on account of the want of timber. For the country is bare; a great part of it is covered with shrubs and produces nothing but the palm. This tree grows in the greatest abundance in Babylonia. . . . . They do not use tiles for their houses, because there are no great rains. (XVI, I, 5.)

"The country is intersected by many rivers, the largest of which are the Euphrates and the Tigris. . . . . The Tigris is navigable upwards from its mouth to Seleucia. . . . . The Euphrates also is navigable up to Babylon. . . . . The Persians, through fear of incursions from without, and for the purpose of preventing vessels from ascending these rivers, constructed artificial cataracts. Alexander, on arriving there, destroyed as many of them as he could. . . . . But he bestowed great care upon the canals; for the Euphrates, at the commencement of summer, overflows. It begins to fill in the spring, when the snow in Armenia melts; the ploughed land, therefore, would be covered with water and be submerged, unless the overflow of the superabundant water were diverted by trenches and canals, as in Egypt the waters of the Nile are diverted. Hence the origin of canals. Great labor is requisite for their maintenance, for the soil is deep, soft and yielding, so that it would easily be swept away by the stream; the fields would be laid bare, the canals filled, and the accumulation of mud would soon obstruct their mouths." (XVI, I, 9.)

§ I. 171 *Schoeni*.

There are discrepancies in the distances given from Apamia to Seleucia. The sum of the distances from Apamia to Phaliga, as given in the text, is 54 schoeni, and that from Phaliga to Seleucia 100, whereas the entire distance is stated as 171.

Müller revises these figures by inserting 7 schoeni at the canal of Semiramis, where there is evidently an omission; and by altering the second section from Phaliga to Seleucia, summarized in the text as 100, to agree with its footing of 110; which added to 61 in the first stage tallies with the 171 of the summary. It is suspected, however, that there are at least two corrections to be made in the local distances; that between Anatho and Thilabus, appearing in the text as 2, may perhaps be 12; while that between Izan and Aipolis, 16 in the text, may be 6. In the absence of archæological explorations of all these sites, it is impossible to determine such questions definitely.

§ 2. APOLLONIATIS: cf. Strabo (anciently Sittacene.)

§ 2. ARTEMITA or Chalasar: cf. Strabo (XVI, I, 17); Ptolemy VI, 1; Peutinger Tables—perhaps the modern Karastar, 7 m. east of Bakuba, where there are extensive ruins. The ancient capital of the Seleucidæ was Apollonia, near Shehrban; under the Parthians, Artemita displaced it.

§ 2. SILLA RIVER, the modern Diala; Ammianus Marcellinus, XXIII, 6. Dialas; Steph. Byz., Delas.

§ 3. CHALONITIS; cf. Strabo, XI, 14, 8, XVI, 1, 1; Pliny, VI, 30, XXVII, 31. Polybius, V, 54.

§ 3. CHALA, the modern Halvan. The Celonæ of earlier writers; here Xerxes located a colony of Bœotians. According to

Masson there are extensive ruins of an ancient city near the modern town.

§ 3. ZAGRUS, now Jebel Tak. The great highway between Assyria and Media led through the gates of Zagrus (Cf. Ritter, *Erdkunde*, IX, 387.)

§ 4. CARINA, the modern Kerent or Kerind.

§ 5. CAMBADENE: For the city of Cambadene (not mentioned in the text) A. V. W. Jackson suggests Kermanshah (34° 20' N., 46° 55' E.) *Persia Past and Present*, 230.

§ 5. BAGISTANA: the text is corrupt, having Baptana. This is Behistun (34° 30' N., 47° 5' E.) near the modern Kermanshah.

§ 5. THE MOUNTAIN OF SEMIRAMIS (Diodorus II, 13) is the modern Tak-i-Bostan. (Cf. Rawlinson, *Third Monarchy*, I.) The rock of Behistun was made a memorial of conquest by many monarchs, Babylonian, Assyrian, Median, Persian and Parthian. The principalin scriptions are of Darius Hystaspes. Others are of the Parthian Gotarzes. Cf. also Tacitus.

§ 6. CONCOBAR: Chaone of Diodorus, Ptolemy and Steph. Byz.—while Polybius has Chauonitis, a province of Media. Abulfeda, Kenkobar; the modern Kungawar, (34°, 38' N., 47° 55' E.) cf. Ritter IX, 345. Jackson, *Persia Past and Present*, 236. Many ruins exist at this site. Diodorus ascribes the shrine to Semiramis. There are colossal ruins at the summit of the hill on which the town stands, which probably represent the ancient temple. (C. Masson.)

§ 6. ADRAPANA; the modern Arteman, on the southern slope of Elwend near its base, well adapted for a royal residence. (Rawlinson, *Third Monarchy*, I.)

§ 6. BATANI; a corrupt reading, Ecbatana being the only possible rendering.

§ 6. TIGRANES the ARMENIAN, ally of Mithridates of Pontus, and enemy of both Rome and Parthia; in his youth a hostage in Parthia, acceded to his throne under promise to cede territory, which he subsequently attacked and reoccupied, and between B. C. 92 and 88 invaded and took possession of Parthian territory in upper Mesopotamia. Cf. Strabo, XI, 14, 15; Justin, XXXVIII, 3, 1; Plutarch, *Lucullus*, 14, 15; Rawlinson, *Sixth Monarchy*, IX. Tigranes died B. C. 55, at the age of 85 (Lucian, *Macrob.* 15.)

§ 6. BATANA; perhaps a corrupt reading; evidently Ecbatana, the Hagmatan of the Medes and Persians, the modern Hamadan, (34°

50′ N., 48° 18′ E.) This is the Achmetha of Ezra VI, 2. See also Judith, I, 1-4. The summer residence of the Persian and Parthian Kings. It was surrounded by seven walls; the citadel was a royal treasury. The splendid palace was sacked and its gold and silver ornaments, to the value of 4000 talents, coined into money by Antiochus the Great of Syria; see Herodotus I, 98; Polybius, X, 27. Diodorus (XVII, 80) says the treasure deposited at Ecbatana was 180,000 talents (about $200,000,000.) Cf. Rawlinson, *Third Monarchy* I.

§ 6. ANAITIS, the Anahita of the Persians, borrowed from Babylonia. The ancient Accadian Ana, god of the sky, became the Semitic Anu, whose female double was Anat, the earth—the female principle—with attributes similar to Ishtar. Sometimes identified with Artemis. Cf. the Nanaia of Elam, (2 Maccabees I, 13-15; Polybius XXXI, II; Josephus, *Ant. Jud*, XII, 9) and the Nana of Babylon. (Harper, *Assyrian and Babylonian Literature*, 116, 245; Roscher, *Lexicon der Griech. u. Röm. Mythologie*, III, 4.) The cult was widespread throughout the Parthian dominions. As to its dissolute customs, cf. Strabo, XI, 8, 12; XI, 14, 16; XII, 3, 37; Plutarch, *Artaxerxes*, 27; also Frazer, *Golden Bough*, (3) I, 16, 37; W. Robertson Smith, *Religion of the Semites*, 325; Sayce, *Hibbert Lectures*, 192. The Annals of Ashurbanipal (668-626 B. C.) speak of the recovery of Nanna from Elam upon his subjugation of that country, "a place not suitable for her," where she "had been angry for 1635 years."

See also Curzon, *Persia*, I, 5; Flandin and Coste, *Perse Ancienne*, I, pl. 20-3; Dieulafoy, *L'Art Antique de la Perse*, V, 7-11.

§ 7. MEDIA RHAGIANA. A very fertile strip between the Elburz range and the salt desert to the south, about 150 miles long, from the Caspian Gates to the modern Kasvin.

§ 7. RHAGA, or Rhages. The name survives in the modern Rei, but the site seems to be some distance N. E., at the modern Kaleh Erij (35° 25′ N., 51° 35′ E.) near Veramin, where there are ruins at the southern base of the Elburz range. According to Arrian, Rhaga was one day's march (about 30 miles) from the Caspian Gates, long an important trade center and the chief residence of the Mazdean priesthood. Scene of the disastrous defeat of Yezdigerd IV, the last of the Sassanian Kings, by the Arabs (A. D. 641). The Rhagæ of Arrian, (*Anab*. III, 20.) Rages (Tobit I,) Ragan (Judith I). The Parthian name of the city was Arsacia (Strabo, XI, 13, 6) Cf. Rawlinson, *Third Monarchy*, I.

§ 7. CHARAX, is probably the modern ruin of Uewanukif, near the Caspian Gates. Both Rhaga and Charax are now represented by the modern Teheran. Charax means "palisade" or "palisaded earthwork." Charax Mediæ is of course not to be confused with Charax Spasini.

§ 7. The MARDI, a poor but warlike people of the Elburz range, were attacked and subdued by Phraates I, soon after his accession in B. C. 181. They were subjects of the Seleucidæ. Seleucus IV (Philopator) then ruling in Syria, was too much weakened by his father's great war with Rome (B. C. 197-190) to offer resistance to the Parthians. Cf. Rawlinson's *Sixth Monarchy*, IV; Justin XLI, 5; Arrian *Anab.* III, 24; Strabo XI, 8, 1 & 8; Herodotus I, 126. This occupation of a strong position west of the Caspian Gates, commanding the Seleucian city of Rhaga, was followed up by the next Parthian king, Mithridates I, who greatly extended his dominions at the expense of the Seleucidæ.

§ 7. CASPIAN MOUNTAIN; This is the Elburz range.

§ 7. CASPIAN GATES, a remarkable pass between Eastern and Western Asia, through which all trade and all military expeditions had to pass. The Caspian Gates were one of the principal strategic points of ancient history, commanding, as they did, the highway between the East and West. At this point the Elburz mountains, which run generally from east to west, send out a long spur south-westerly into the desert and in this spur there are several openings through which travelers may go to avoid the detour into the desert. The modern route runs through the Girduni Sudurrah pass, which Curzon interprets as Sirdarah—Ser-i-dareh, ("Head of the valley"). The descriptions of the pass given in the classic writers show clearly that the modern route is not the one then used, but that the Caspian Gates of that period were probably identical with the Teng-i-Suluk, about four miles north of the present route. (35° 20′ N., 52° E.) Cf. Curzon, *Persia* I, 293-5 and authorities there quoted; also Pliny, VI, 14.

The name was derived from the tribe of the Caspii, who gave their name also to the Caspian Sea, known to Greek writers as the Hyrcanian Sea; cf. Rawlinson, *Sixth Monarchy*, IV.

§ 8. CHOARENA. The name survives in the modern Chawar.

§ 8. APAMIA. Cf. Strabo, XI, 9, 1, XI, 13, 6; Ptolemy, VI, 5. A Greek city founded by the Macedonians.

§ 11. ASTAUENA; Cf. Ptolemy, VI, 9; also Asbana Urbs of the Peutinger Tables, XII, C.

§ 11. ARSACES, founder of the Parthian dynasty, chieftain of a tribe of Iranian nomads east of the Caspian, who asserted independence of Diodotus, King of Bactria, who had separated from the Seleucid empire; Seleucus II, with civil war and a war with Egypt, could not prevent the loss of both provinces. Arsaces was proclaimed king in 248 B. C. He and his successors rapidly absorbed the Seleucid dominions, and by 129 B. C. their rule extended to the Euphrates. Their following included Scythian, Parthian and Greek elements. (Eusebius *Chron.* i, 207. *Canon.* ii, 120; Appian, *Syr.* 65; Arrian, *Parthica*; Justin xli, 4, 5; Rawlinson, *Sixth Monarchy*; Encycl. Brit. XX, 870–1. Wrode, *Catalogue of the Coins of Parthia in the British Museum.*)

§ 11. ASAAC (probably *Arsak*), now Kuchan in the upper Atrek valley. (37° 8′N., 58° 20′E.)

§ 11. EVERLASTING FIRE; The Arsacid dynasty embraced the Zarathushtrian religion; their language "a mixture of Scythian and Median" (Iranian) is called Pehlevi (a later form of *Parthawa.*) Pliny (II, 109) speaks of the naphtha springs of "Austacene Parthiæ."

§ 12. PARTHAUNISA or NISAEA, the modern Naishapur. (36° 12′ N. 58° 50′ E.)

§ 13. APAUARCTICENA; Cf. Pliny vi, 16. This is the Zapaortenon of Justin, xli, 5.

§ 13. APAUARCTICA; Cf. ARTACANA of Ptolemy. Possibly Dara, built by the Parthian King Tiridates about B. C. 230 as his residence, supplanting the Greek city of Hecatompylos; very near the modern Meshed.

§ 14. ANTIOCHIA MARGIANA; Cf. Pliny VI, 18; the modern Mervrud. (35° 50′ N., 63° 5′ E.).

§ 15. ARIA. This was the Haraina of the *Vendidad.*

§ 15. ARTACAUAN; Cf. Artacoana of Arrian, *Anab.* III, 25; Pliny VI, 25; Artacaëna, Strabo, XI, 10, 1; Articaundra, Ptolemy VI, 17. This site was evidently very near to or almost identical with the modern Herat.

§ 15. ALEXANDRIA OF THE ARII; Cf. Pliny VI, 21. Strabo, XI, 8, 9; 10, 1; Ammianus Marcellinus XXIII, 6, 69; the modern Herat. (34° 25′ N., 62° 15′ E.).

§ 16. PHRA, the modern Fara; the Phrada of Steph. Byz. (32° 20' N., 62° 9' E.).

§ 16. GARI may be the modern GIRISHK, Cf. the Harakhraiti of the *Vendidad* (?).

§ 16. NIA; the modern Neh. (31° 30' N., 60° 5' E.).

§ 17. ZARANGIANA, the Sarangians of Herodotus (III, 93), the 14th satrapy of Darius; the Zarangæans of Arrian (*Anab.* III, 25); the Drangians of Diodorus (XVII, 78) (?). Pliny puts the Sarangæ and the Drangæ side by side (VI, 27). The name signifies "lake dwellers," referring to Lake Helmund; *zareh*=lake. Cf. Strabo XV, 2, 8.

§ 18. SACASTANA of the Scythian Sacæ. This is the modern Seistan. The Sacæ, formerly residents of Central Asia, were driven out by the Yue-chi and forced across the Pamirs into Bactria. About 100 B. C. the Yue-chi followed them, overran Bactria and upper India, and established the Kushan monarchy. The Sacæ, driven before them, occupied the country around Lake Helmund, and overran the lower Indus valley, and the Cutch and Cambay coasts of Western India. They were tributary in some degree to the Parthian monarchy, and in Indian history they appear as the "Indo-Parthians." Gondophares of the Acts of St. Thomas was an Indo-Parthian prince; the *Periplus*, about 80 A. D., mentions his quarrelling successors in the Indus delta, and a Saka satrap, Nahapāna, who established a powerful state in the Cambay district and instituted the Saka era of 78 A. D. Cf. Strabo, XI, 8, 2-5. Schoff, *Periplus of the Erythræan Sea*, 184-7.

§ 18. PARAETACENA: Cf. Herodotus I, 101; Ptolemy VI, 4.

The word is Persian in origin and means simply "mountainous."

§ 18. MIN. This seems to have been the Saka name for their race. The name appears in two cities in India mentioned in the *Periplus* as *Min-nagara*, "city of the Min": one in the Indus delta and the other in the Cambay region. Cf. Schoff, *Periplus*, 165, 180.

§ 18. SIGAL, the royal residence. Cf. Nimrus of the Rustam story in the *Shah Nama*. The location of the site is not determined.

Concerning this fertile delta of the Helmund, Major Sykes, (*Ten Thousand Miles in Persia*, 361) says:

"Before entering the province of Sistán it may perhaps not be out of place to outline the various interesting historical and physical problems by which we are confronted.

"In the Sháh Náma Sistán is the home of the famous family of champions, who seated the Keiánian dynasty on the throne of Persia. Their most brilliant scion was Rustam, whose matchless daring forms the main theme of Firdusi's great epic, and who is as much the national hero to-day as he was a thousand years or more ago, everything in Persia that is not understood, such as the Sassanian rock sculptures at Persepolis, being attributed to this champion, who like the Homeric heroes, was as mighty a trencherman as warrior, and almost equally respected for his prowess in both fields.

"At the period referred to above, Sagistán, as Sistán was then called, practically meant the low country to the west of Kandahár, Zabulistán being the name for the upland country, now the home of the Berbers. During the latter years of Rustam—he lived well over a century—the Persian capital was shifted from the banks of the Helmund to Fárs, and in due course history takes the place of legend.

"With regard to the historical existence of Rustam, I think we may at all events admit that there was a champion or a family of champions, who led the hosts of Iran, and furthermore, that as their history is given so circumstantially almost down to historical times, there is every probability that their exploits have a substratum of truth. Moreover, in those days, a man bigger and heavier than his adversaries, always inspired a very wholesome fear, for not only could he deal deadlier blows, but, equally important, he could carry heavier armour; in fact he was like a battleship and his opponents resembled cruisers.

"The Sarangians, mentioned by Herodotus as belonging to the 14th satrapy, occupied Sistán during the reign of Darius, and the Greek historians who narrated the conquests of Alexander the Great, gave the name of Drangiana to what is now, roughly speaking, Southern Afghanistan. This province was traversed by the world-conqueror on his way to Bactria and by Krateros on his march from Karachi to Karmania. But the most ancient traveller who actually visited and described these provinces, albeit very briefly, is Isidorus of Charax, who was a contemporary of Augustus, and whose account is of such value that I quote it in a footnote.* We thus see that Fara and Neh were important towns, while Gari may be Girishk. Zarangia is the same as Sarangia, and includes Persian Sistán. The town of Zirra is apparently the same word which still survives in the name of the great lagoon mentioned below.

"Sakastani, or the land of the Sakæ, is evidently the same word as the Sistán of today. The Sakæ have disappeared from this part

---

*This is §16 of the *Mansiones Parthicae* or *Parthian Stations*.

of Asia, but I understand that the theory connecting them with the Saxons is held in certain quarters."

Major Sykes (*Ten Thousand Miles in Persia*, p. 14) says:

"Neh, first mentioned as Nie by Isidorus of Charax, is undoubtedly a site of great antiquity, and must have been a place of importance, lying as it does on the direct line between Bandar Abbás and the Khorasán, and within the first cultivated area struck by caravans after leaving Narmáshir. At the present time nine routes radiate from the town. Ancient Neh, which no traveller had hitherto discovered, is undoubtedly what is known as Kala Sháh Duzd, three miles to the east of the more modern fort; it is built on a hill only accessible on the west side, and is carefully guarded by numerous sangars. The track about half-way up enters the line of bastioned wall by passing under a little fort which was almost a duplicate of Kala Zarri. Above, lying up the steep hill-side, were thousands of houses, built of unhewn stone fitted together with mortar, the summit being some 600 feet above the plain. The other faces are perpendicular, but the water-supply seemed insufficient, there being only tanks, so far as could be seen. The area covered was quite four acres, and these are certainly the most important ruins which I have examined in Eastern Persia.

"Legend has it that Shah Duzd, or King Thief, forced Zál to pay tribute, until Rustam grew up, when the overlord was challenged to single combat. All their weapons having been exhausted, they wrestled until, by mutual consent, a halt was made for refreshment. Rustam of subtlety indulged sparingly, but his less careful opponent drank his fill, and was easily worsted, thereby sealing his own doom.

"Neh grows ample supplies for its own consumption, but as it feeds all the caravans passing in other directions, it imports grain largely from Sistán; this accounts for the number of its mills. Its population is perhaps 5000 or rather less."

§ 18. ALEXANDRIA. It is very possible that both Alexandria and Alexandropolis in this §18 are interpolations of some scribe and that they are intended for the Alexandropolis of §19, the modern Kandahar.

§ 19. ARACHOSIA. (White India.) Substantially the modern Afghanistan. Cf. Lassen, *Indische Alterthumskunde*, 1,434. The modern Arab name is Arrokadsch. Cf. Strabo, III, 10, 1.

§ 19. ALEXANDROPOLIS, the modern Kandahar. (31° 39' N., 65° 48' E.) See Arrian, *Anab*. III, 28.

§ 19. ARACHOTUS RIVER, the modern Argandáb.

Strabo says of this region generally (XV, 2-8):

"The greater part of the country inhabited by the Icthyophagi is on a level with the sea. No trees except palms and a kind of thorn, and the tamarisk grow there. There is also a scarcity of water and of food produced by cultivation. Both they and their cattle subsist upon fish and are supplied by rain water and wells. The flesh of the animals has the smell of fish. Their dwellings are built with the bones of large whales and shells, the ribs furnishing beams and supports, and the jaw-bones door-ways. The vertebral bones serve as mortars in which fish, which have been previously dried in the sun, are pounded. Of this, with the addition of flour, cakes are made; for they have grinding mills (for corn), although they have no iron. This, however, is not so surprising, because it is possible for them to import it from other parts. But how do they hollow out the mills again when worn away? With the same stones, they say, with which their arrows and javelins, which are hardened in the fire are sharpened. Some fish are dressed in ovens, but the greater part is eaten raw. The fish are taken in nets made of the bark of the palm.

"Above the Icthyophagi is situated Gedrosia (Makran), a country less exposed to the heat of the sun than India, but more so than the rest of Asia. As it is without fruits and water, except in summer, it is not much better than the country of the Icthyophagi. But it produces aromatics, particularly nard and myrrh, in such quantity that the army of Alexander used them on the march for tent coverings and beds; they thus breathed an air full of odors, and at the same time more salubrious.

"The summer was purposely chosen for leaving India, for at that season it rains in Gedrosia, and the rivers and wells are filled, but in winter they fail. The rain falls in the higher parts to the north, and near the mountains; when the rivers fill, the plains near the sea are watered, and the wells are also filled. Alexander sent persons before him into the desert country to dig wells and to prepare stations for himself and his fleet.

"Having separated his forces into three divisions, he set out with one division through Gedrosia, keeping at the utmost from the sea not more than 500 stadia, in order to secure the coast for his fleet; but he frequently approached the sea-side, although the beach was impracticable and rugged. The second division he sent forward under the command of Craterus through the interior, with a view of reducing Ariana, and of proceeding to the same places to which he was himself directing his march. The third division, the fleet, he intrusted to

Nearchus and Onesicritus, his master pilot, giving them orders to take up convenient positions in following him, and to sail along the coast parallel to his line of march."

In another section (XV, 2, 5), Strabo observes:

"Nearchus says that while Alexander was on his march, he himself commenced his voyage, in the autumn, about the achronical rising of the Pleiades, the wind not being before favorable. The Barbarians however, taking courage at the departure of the king, became daring, and attempted to throw off their subjection, attacked them and endeavored to drive them out of the country. But Craterus set out from the Hydaspes, and proceeded through the country of the Arachoti and of the Drangæ into Carmania.

"Alexander was greatly distressed throughout the whole march, as his road lay through a barren country. The supplies of provisions which he obtained came from a distance and were scanty and unfrequent, so much so that the army suffered greatly from hunger, the beasts of burden dropped down and the baggage was abandoned, both on the march and in the camp. The army was saved by eating dates and the marrow of the palm tree.

"Alexander, however (says Nearchus), although acquainted with the hardships of the enterprise, was ambitious of conducting this large army in safety, as a conqueror, through the same country where, according to the prevailing report, Semiramis escaped by flight from India with about twenty and Cyrus with about seven men."

This is the modern trade route from Afghanistan by Lake Helmund and Kerman to the head of the Persian Gulf.

Strabo, (XI, 8, 8-9) further observes:

"Eratosthenes says that the Bactrians lie along the Arachoti and Massagetæ on the west near the Oxus, and that the Sacæ and Sogdiani, through the whole extent of their territory, are opposite to India, but the Bactrii in part only, for the greater part of their country lies parallel to the Parapamisus; that the Sacæ and Sogdiani are separated by the Iaxartes, and the Sogdiani and Bactriani by the Oxus; that Tapyri occupy the country between the Hyrcani and Arii; that around the shores of the sea, next to the Hyrcani, are Amardi, Anariacæ, Cadusii, Albani, Caspii, Vitii, and perhaps other tribes extending as far as the Scythians; that on the other side of the Hyrcani are Derbices, that the Caducii are contiguous both to the Medes and Matiani below the Parachoathras.

"These are the distances which he gives:

	Stadia
From the Caspian Sea to the Cyrus about	1,800
Thence to the Caspain Gates	5,600
Thence to Alexandria in the territory of the Arii	6,400
Thence to the city Bactra, which is called also Zariaspa	3,870
Thence to the river Iaxartes, which Alexander reached, about	5,000
Making a total of	22,670

"He also assigns the following distances from the Caspian Gates to India:

	Stadia
To Hecatompylos	1,960
To Alexandreia in the country of the Arii (Ariana)	4,530
Thence to Prophthasia in Dranga	1,600
(or according to others, 1,500)	
Thence to the city Arachoti	4,120
Thence to Ortospana on the three roads from Bactra	2,000
Thence to the confines of India	1,000
Which together amount to	15,300"

The location of these tribes shows clearly the race migrations that occurrod between the time of Eratosthenes and that of Isidore. The Sacæ, which he has east of the Iaxartes, the modern Syr-Daria, Isidore has settled in the Helmund Valley. The Sogdiani, whom Eratosthenes places between the Sacæ and the Oxus (the modern Amu-Daria) have likewise moved south and west and in Isidore's time are under the dominion of the Kushan kings in Bactria.

The Arachosii appear in the Periplus about A. D. 80 as one of the tribes inland from the Indus Valley, north of whom were the "nation of the Bactrians", by which was meant the Kushan dominions.

The *Periplus* has an interesting note of the commercial importance of the Greek civilization in that regin, when it speaks of the silver coins of the Greek dynasty in Bactria as still current in the ports of the Cambay region, more than 200 years after they were issued.

The fact that through the province of Arachosia runs one of the principal trade routes between Persia and India made it always politically important and commercially prosperous.

The following references from the *Periplus* are of interest in connection with the itinerary of Isidore:

(Quoted from Schoff, *The Periplus of the Erythræan Sea*, pp. 41, 183, 189.)

(P. 41). "The country inland from Barygaza is inhabited by numerous tribes, such as the Arattii, the Arachosii, the Gandaræi and the people of Poclais, in which is Bucephalus Alexandria. Above these is the very warlike nation of the Bactrians, who are ruled by a Kushan king.* And Alexander, setting out from these parts, penetrated to the Ganges, leaving aside Damirica and the southern part of India; and to the present day ancient drachmæ are current in Barygaza, coming from this country, bearing inscriptions in Greek letters, and the devices of those who reigned after Alexander, Apollodotus and Menander."

(P. 183). "ARATTII. This is a Prakrit form of the Sanscrit *Arāshtra*, who were a people of the Punjab; in fact the name *Arātta* is often synonymous with the Panjāb in Hindu literature."

(P. 183). "ARACHOSII. This people occupied the country around the modern Kandahar (31° 27' N., 65° 43' E.). McCrindle (*Ancient India*, 88) says 'Arachosia extended westward beyond the meridian of Kandahar, and was skirted on the east by the river Indus. On the north it stretched to the western section of the Hindu Kush and on the south to Gedrosia. The province was rich and populous, and the fact that it was traversed by one of the main routes by which Persia communicated with India added greatly to its importance.'"

(P. 183). "GANDARAEI (Sanskrit, Gāndhāra). This people dwelt on both sides of the Kabul River, above its junction with the Indus; the modern Peshāwur district. In earlier times they extended east of the Indus, where their eastern capital was located—*Takshasilā*, a large and prosperous city, called by the Greeks *Taxila*.

"(See also Holdich, *Gates of India*, 99, 114, 179, 185; Vincent Smith, *Early History of India*, 32, 43, 50, 52, 54; Foucher, *Notes sur la Géographie Ancienne du Gāndhāra*.)

"The trade-route briefly referred to in the mention of Gāndhāra and Pushkalāvati was that leading to Bactria, whence it branched westward to the Caspian and the Euphrates, and eastward through Turkestan to China, the 'Land of This' of § 64 of the *Periplus*."

(P. 189). "CASPAPYRA. This is the Greek form of the Sanskrit *Kāsyapapura*, 'city of the Kāsyapa.' The same word survives in the modern Kashmir, which is from the Sanscrit *Kāsyapamata* (pronounced *Pamara*), and meaning 'home of the Kāsyapa' (one of the 'previous Buddhas'). According to the division of the Greek geographers, Gāndhāra was the country below Kabul, while

---

* An amended reading suggested by Kennedy, and according well with historical facts and probabilities.

Kāsyapamata was the adjoining district in India proper. (See Lassen, I, 142; II, 631.)

"It was from a town named Caspapyra, that Scylax of Caryanda began his voyage of discovery at the command of the Persian king Darius. The story is given by Herodotus (IV, 44). He refers to the place as being 'in the Pactyan land,' and Hecatæus calls it 'a city of the Gandaræans.' It could not have been far above the modern Attock (33° 53' N., 72° 15' E.). Vincent Smith (*Early History*, 32) doubts the connection of the name with Kashmir; but while outside the present limits of that district, it is not impossible that its earlier extension was wider. The fact that the *Periplus* distinguishes it from Gāndhāra points in that direction."

§ 20. This passage from Isidore, quoted by Athenæus, seems to be from his complete work, whereas the *Parthian Stations*, as we have it, is rather a condensed summary.

§ 21-33. These fragments, quoted by Pliny in his *Natural History*, indicate that Isidore was the author of a considerable work on geography, now lost.

§ 34. ARTAXERXES, possibly Artaxerxes Ochus of the Achæmenid line, who was poisoned in 338 B. C. by his general, Bagoas; but this seems rather to be some Artaxerxes of the tributary kingdom of Persia in Parthian times. The statements of Isidore do not accord with the fate of Ochus, and the event is said to have occurred in the generation before Isidore, which was three centuries later than the Achæmenid period.

§ 35. GOÆSUS. (Compare *Geez*, the ancient language of the Abyssinians), King of the Omanitæ in the Incense Land. This lies in South Arabia, on either side of the Kuria Muria or Zenobian Islands. Glaser has quoted inscriptions showing that after an alliance between the Incense Land and the Sabæans, their enemies, the Homerites and the Chatramotitæ were victorious, the latter seizing the rich and productive frankincense territory, and the Abaseni migrating to the coast of Africa, where they established the kingdom of Abyssinia, long a bitter enemy of the Homerites in Arabia. Goæsus must have been one of the last kings of the Abaseni in Arabia. Cf. Glaser, *Die Abessinier iu Arabien und Afrika*, 90-92; Schoff, *The Periplus of the Erythræan Sea*, 116-143.

PARALLEL PASSAGES FROM THE CHINESE ANNALS

(Quoted from Hirth, *China and the Roman Orient.*)
Shih-chi. ch. 123, written about 91 B.C.

"When the first embassy was sent from China to An-hsi (=Ar-sak, Parthia) the King of Parthia ordered 20,000 cavalry to meet them on the eastern frontier. The eastern frontier was several thousand *li* (practically the same as *stadia*, 10 to the mile) from the King's capital. Proceeding to the north one came across several tens of cities, with very many inhabitants, allied to that country. After the Chinese embassy had returned they sent forth an embassy to follow the Chinese embassy, to come and see the extent and greatness of the Chinese Empire. They offered to the Chinese court large birds' eggs, and jugglers from Li-kan (=Re-kam, Petra)."

Ch'ien-han-shu, ch. 96a, written about 90 A.D. and embracing events from 206 B.C. to 25 A.D.

"The King of the country of Parthia rules at the city of P'an-tu (=Parthuva, Hecatompylos); its distance from Ch'ang-an is 11,-600 *li*. The country is not subject to a *tu-hu* (Chinese governor in Central-Asiatic possessions). It bounds north on K'ang-chü, east on Wu-i-shan-li (Arachosia), west on T'iao-chih (Chaldaea). The soil, climate, products, and popular customs are the same as those of Wu-i and Chi-pin (Kashmir). They also make coins of silver, which have the king's face on the obverse, and the face of his consort on the reverse. When the king dies, they cast new coins. They have the *ta-ma-ch'uo* (ostrich). Several hundred small and large cities are subject to it, and the country is several thousand *li* in extent; that is a very large country. It lies on the banks of the Kwei-shui (Oxus). The wagons and ships of their merchants go to the neighboring countries. They write on parchment, and draw up documents in rows running sideways."

Ibid. ch. 96a.

"When the emperor Wu-ti (140-86 B.C.) first sent an embassy to Parthia, the King ordered a general to meet him on the eastern frontier with 20,000 cavalry. The eastern frontier was several thousand *li* distant from the King's capital. Proceeding to the north one came across several tens of cities, the inhabitants of which were allied with that country. As they sent forth an embassy to follow the Chinese embassy, they came to see the country of China. They offered to the Chinese court large birds'-eggs, and jugglers from

Petra, at which His Majesty was highly pleased. In the east of Parthia are the Ta-yueh-chi (Tochari)."

Ibid. ch. 96a.

"Wu-i-shan-li (apparently includes both Arachosia and Persia) is in the west, conterminous with Li-Kan (Arabia Petræa) and T'iao-chih (Chaldaea).* Going somewhat over 100 days you come to the country of T'iao-chih, bordering on the Western sea, hot and low, but growing rice in fields. There are large birds, eggs, resembling urns. The country is densely populated; it used to be governed by petty rulers, but Parthia, reducing them to vassalage, made it a dependent state. They have clever jugglers. From T'iao-chih by water you may go west over 100 days to come near the place where the sun sets, they say."

Hou-han-shu, ch. 88; partly written during the 5th century A. D. and embracing the period 25 to 220 A. D.

"From Parthia you go west 3,400 *li* to the country of A-man (Akhmatan, Ecbatana); from A-man you go west 3,600 *li* to the country of Ssŭ-pin (Ctesiphon); from Ssŭ-pin you go south, crossing a river, and again southwest to the country of Yü-lo (Hira, the Babylonian Lake at the head of the Pallacopas canal) 960 *li*, the extreme west frontier of Parthia; from here you travel south by sea, and so reach Ta-ts'in (Syria). In this country there are many of the precious and rare things of the western sea.

"The city of the country of T'iao-chih (Chaldaea) is situated on a peninsula (*shan*, also meaning hill or island); its circumference is over forty *li* and it borders on the western sea (Hira Lake). The waters of the sea crookedly surround it. In the south, east and northeast, the road is cut off; only in the north-west there is access to it by a land-road. The country is hot and low. It produces lions, rhinoceros, zebu, peacocks, and large birds (ostriches) whose eggs are like urns. If you turn to the north and then towards the east again go on horseback some 60 days, you come to Parthia, to which afterwards it became subject as a vasal state under a military governor who had control of all the small cities.

"The country of Parthia has its residence at the city of Ho-tu (Vologesia, Hecatompylos?); it is 25,000 *li* distant from Lo-yang (Singanfu). In the north it bounds on K'ang-chü, and in the south, on Wu-i-shan-li. The size of the country is several thousand *li*. There are several hundred small cities with a vast number of inhabitants

---

*The two names, Dr. Hirth suggests, may have denoted the western and eastern parts, respectively, of the Seleucid dominions.

and soldiers. On its eastern frontier is the city of Mu-lu (Mōuru, Merv) which is called Little Parthia. It is 20,000 *li* distant from Lo-yang. In the first year of Chang-ho, of the Emperor Chang-ti (87 A. D.) they sent an embassy offering lions and *fu-pa*. The *fu-pa* has the shape of a unicorn, but has no horn. In the 9th year of Yung-yüan of Ho-ti (97 A. D.) the general Pan Ch'ao sent Kan-ying as an ambassador to Ta-ts'in, who arrived in T'iao-chih, on the coast of the great sea. When about to take his passage across the sea, the sailors of the western frontier of Parthia told Kan-ying: 'The sea is vast and great; with favorable winds it is possible to cross within three months; but if you meet slow winds, it may also take you two years. It is for this reason that those who go to sea take on board a supply of three years' provisions. There is something in the sea which is apt to make a man home-sick, and several have thus lost their lives.' When Kan-ying heard this, he stopped . . . .

"In the 13th year (101 A. D.) the king of Parthia, Man-k'ü (Pacorus?) again offered as tribute lions and large birds from T'iao-chih (ostriches), which henceforth were named *An-hsi-chiao* (Parthian birds) . . . . .

"The country of Ta-ts'in (Syria) is also called Li-chien (Li-kin, Re-kam, Petra) and, as being situated on the western part of the sea, Hai-hsi-kuo (country of the western part of the sea). Its territory amounts to several thousand *li*; it contains over four hundred cities, and of dependent states there are several times ten . . . . . The country contains much gold, silver and rare precious stones, ... corals, amber, glass, ... gold-embroidered rugs and thin silk cloth of various colors. They make gold-colored cloth and asbestos cloth. They further have 'fine cloth,' also called 'down of the water sheep'; it is made from the cocoons of wild silk-worms. They collect all kinds of fragrant substances, the juice of which they boil into *su-ho* (storax). All the rare gems of other foreign countries come from there. They make coins of gold and silver. Ten units of silver are worth one of gold. They traffic by sea with Parthia and India, the profit of which trade is ten-fold. They are honest in their transactions, and there are no double prices. . . . Their kings always desired to send embassies to China, but the Parthians wished to carry on trade with them in Chinese silks, and it is for this reason that they were cut off from communication. This lasted till the ninth **year of** the Yen-hsi period during the Emperor Huan-ti's reign **(166 A. D.)** when the king of Ta-ts'in, An-tun (Marcus Aurelius **Antoninus)** sent an embassy who from the frontier of Jih-nan (Annam) offered ivory, rhinoceros horns and tortoise shell. From that time dates the direct intercourse with this country. The list of their tribute contained no jewels whatever, which fact throws doubt on the tradition.*

"It is further said that, coming from the land-road of Parthia, you make a round at sea and, taking a northern turn, come out from the western part of the sea, whence you proceed to Ta-ts'in.† One is not alarmed by robbers, but the road becomes unsafe by fierce tigers and lions who will attack passengers, and unless these be traveling in caravans of a hundred men or more, or be protected by military equipment, they may be devoured by those beasts. . . . .

"The articles made of rare precious stones produced in this country are sham curiosities and mostly not genuine, whence they are not here mentioned."

Sung-shu, ch. 97, written about 500 A.D. and embracing the period 420-478 A.D.

"As regards Ta-ts'in (Syria) and T'ien-chu (India), far out on the western ocean, we have to say that, although the envoys of the two Han dynasties have experienced the special difficulties of this road, yet traffic in merchandise has been effected, and goods have been sent out to the foreign tribes, the force of winds driving them far away acroas the waves of the sea. There are lofty ranges of mountains quite different from those we know and a great variety of populous tribes having different names and bearing uncommon designations, they being of a class quite different from our own. All the precious things of land and water come from there, as well as the gems made of rhinoceros horns and chrysoprase, serpent pearls and asbestos cloth, there being innumerable varieties of these curiosities; and also the doctrine of the abstraction of mind in devotion to the lord of the world (Buddha)—all this having caused navigation and trade to be extended to those parts."

Wei-shu, ch. 102, written before 572 A.D. and embracing the period 386-556 A.D.

"It is said that from the western boundary of Parthia, following the crooked shape of the sea-coast, you can also go to Ta-ts'in, bending around over 10,000 li."

---

*These were probably merchants trading from the East African coast, and not official ambassadors.

† This trade route follows the overland route through the Caspian Gates to Ctesiphon and Seleucia, thence to Hira Lake and the head of the Persian Gulf, thence by ship around Arabia to Leucē Comē, the Nabatæan Red Sea port, and overland to the capital, Petra.

A MODERN ACCOUNT

The following modern descriptions of Persia and its trade-routes are of interest in connection with the itinerary of Isidore:
(Quoted from Curzon, *Persia*, I, 50-1, and 264.)

"From Bagdad to the Persian frontier, five miles beyond the Turkish station of Khanikin is ninety miles, the road running for the most part over a level desert and the halting-places being as follows: Beni Saad or Orta Khan (15 miles), Yakubish (14), Shahrabad (26), Kizil Robat (18), Khanikin (17). There is no postal service, and the traveler, who must engage his baggage animals at Bagdad, halts in *khans* (the Turkish equivalent to caravanserais) and rest-houses. After passing through the custom-house on the Persian border he finds the following route extended before him:

"Name of Station	Distance in farsakhs	Approx. distance in miles
Khanikin (1000 ft.)	—	—
Kasr-i-Shirin (1700 ft)	6	18
Sarpul	5	18
Kerind (5250 ft.)	8	29
Harunabad	6	20
Mahidasht	6	22
Kermanshah (5000 ft.)	4	14
Bisitun (Behistun)	6	21
Sahneh	4	16
Kangavar	5	18
Saidabad	6	23
Hamadan	6	25
Mili Gird	7	25
Zerreh	4	16
Nuvaran	9	32
Shamiran	4	14
Khushkek	5	19
Khanabad	6	22
Robat Kerim	8	32
Teheran (3800 ft.)	7 (112)	28 (412)

"The total distance between Bagdad and Teheran is thus 90 + 408 miles, or close upon 500 miles.

"This journey is one of threefold and exceptional interest. It crosses the mighty Zagros range between Khanikin and Kermanshah, the steepest part of the pass, known as the Teng-i-Girra, between Sarpul and Kerind, being fully comparable with the *kotals* of the Bushire-Shiraz line, in winter, frequently impassable from snow. By this ascent the traveler is brought up from the level plains of Assyria and Chaldæa to the great Iranian plateau, which he does not again quit until he leaves Persia. Secondly, he passes through the important and flourishing Persian cities of Kermanshah and Hamadan . . . . which are situated in exceedingly productive tracts of country. Lastly, at Bisitun and at Tak-i-Bostan (four miles from Kermanshah) he encounters some of the most celebrated remains of Persian antiquity; and in the rock carvings, sculptures and inscriptions which look down upon him from the chiselled surface of the mountain side, he both reads a tale of bygone splendor and observes the most important historical document, albeit in stone, next to the Damietta Stone, that has been discovered and deciphered in this century . . . ."

"Nishapur . . . . . . is the meeting point of several important roads in addition to the two from Meshed. On the south a road comes in from Turshiz, and on the north a track runs via Madan

IN A PERSIAN CARAVANSERAI, WHICH IS MUCH THE SAME THING AS THE PARTHIAN "STATION"

(where are the turquoise mines) to Kuchan; while in a more westerly direction stretches the old, long-forgotten trade route to the Caspian, which is believed to have been a link in the great chain of overland connection in the middle ages between China and India and the European continent. It ran from Nishapur to the Arab city of Isferayin in the plain of the same name, then struck westwards and passing through the mountains of the defile known as the Dahaneh-i-

Gurgan, through which the river Gurgan forces its way, descended the slope to the Caspian. The stages on this route are recorded on the itineraries of Isidore of Charax and of El Istakhri, and the caravanserais built by Shah Abbas the Great are still standing, though in ruins."

TRADE ROUTES OF MODERN PERSIA.

Curzon, *Persia*, II, 583-4.

Route	No. of Stages or Days
1. Julfa—Tabriz	4
2. Tabriz—Teheran (via Mianeh, Zinjan, Kazvin)	14-16
3. Teheran—Ispahan (via Kum, Kashan)	10-12
4. Ispahan—Shiraz (via Kumisheh, Yezdikhast, Dehbid,)	12
Ispahan—Shiraz (via the summer route from Yezdikhast)	10
5. Shiraz—Bushire (via Kazerun)	10
6. Teheran—Moshed via Semnan, Shahrud, Nishapur)	22
7. Teheran—Resht (via Kazvin)	9-10
8. Teheran—Bagdad (via Hamadan, Kermanshah, Khanikin)	24
9. Teheran—Meshed-i-Ser	6
10. Teheran—Astrabad (via Sari)	14
11. Ispahan—Yezd	10
12. Kashan—Kerman	25
13. Yezd—Kerman	12
14. Kerman—Bam	11
15. Kerman—Bandar Abbas	20
16. Tabriz—Astara (via Ardebil)	7
17. Tabriz—Resht (summer route via Masullah and Fumen)	12
18. Tabriz—Bagdad (via Suleimanieh)	20
19. Hamadan—Sinna	4
20. Hamadan—Shushter	15
21. Resht—Astrabad	14

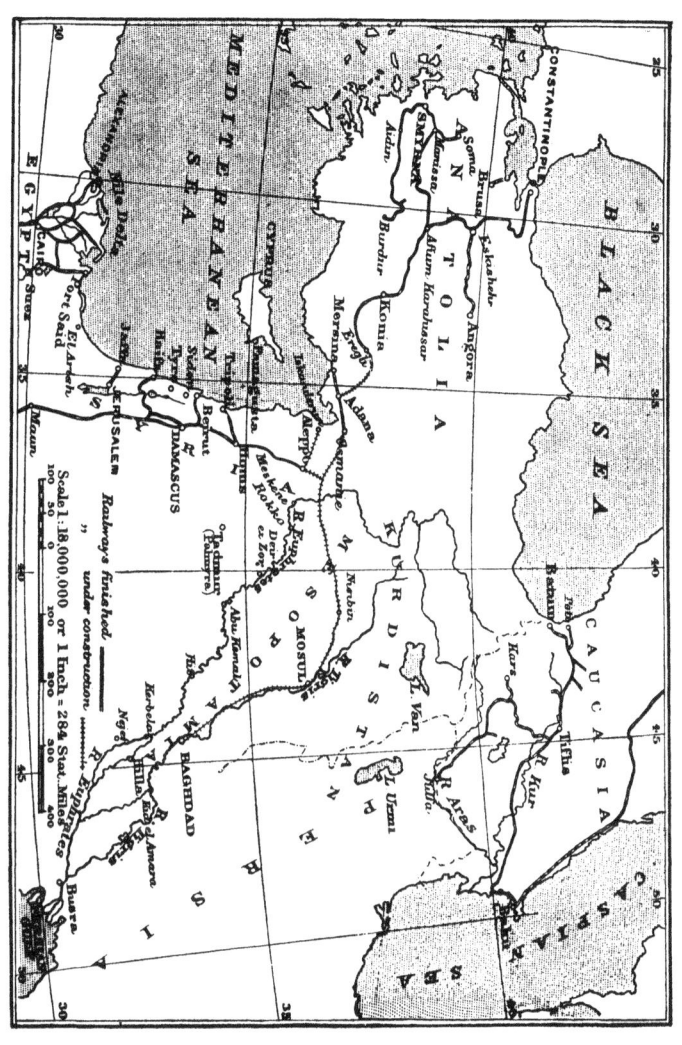

The above map, reproduced from the Geographical Journal, shows modern railway routes in Asia Minor, Syria and Mesopotamia, and is therefore of interest in connection with the itinerary of Isidore.

www.ingramcontent.com/pod-product-compliance
Lightning Source LLC
Chambersburg PA
CBHW071802040426
42446CB00012B/2666